Papers From the

*West Virginia University
Conference on*

Computer Applications
in Music

GERALD LEFKOFF, Editor

WEST VIRGINIA UNIVERSITY LIBRARY
MORGANTOWN, WEST VIRGINIA
1967

McClain Printing Company
Parsons, West Virginia

The publication of this book was
made possible by a grant from the

WEST VIRGINIA UNIVERSITY
FOUNDATION

A publication of the University's 100th Anniversary Year

Contents

Introduction

The volume and scope of musical endeavors in which computers are employed is rapidly increasing and may be expected to continue to do so. Some of the general areas in music in which computers are being used include library services, music printing and editing, analysis of music, solving of theoretical problems, composition and electronic sound generation. The dissemination of information concerning these activities is reaching many musicians through our professional journals and papers and discussions at professional meetings. However, there are a number of interested persons who may be served by some concentrated attention to this topic. Therefore, West Virginia University sponsored on its campus a conference on computer applications in music on April 29 and 30, 1966, and is here publishing the papers presented at that meeting. It is hoped that these papers may, in addition to the message which each conveys, combine to suggest the significance of computer applications for the advancement of musical art and scholarship.

When the speakers were invited to participate and topics selected, an effort was made to include representative work from as many areas as possible. Some areas, however, were unavoidably omitted or received scant mention. The paper by Charles Cook is not on music itself but on the computer in general and is included particularly for the convenience of those who have little or no experience with computers.

Although computer-implemented work in music as such is no longer novel, and although there has been some notable progress and achievement in this field, we are still at a threshold or just a few paces beyond, where we can foresee what may be within reach and the significance and seriousness of the problems both technical and philosophical which must be resolved. It has often been noted that the best use of the computer is not simply as a labor saving device for the automation of established activities, but a means of engaging in activities which depend upon the special capabilities of the computer. In music as in other fields computer-implemented activities should not in most cases replace or render obsolete established non-computer activities. It may nevertheless have an indirect impact upon non-computer activities by influencing ever changing modes of thought, attitudes toward knowledge and art, and through its contribution to the development of new knowledge itself.

Gerald Lefkoff

Music Bibliography and the Computer

by
Barry S. Brook

Hydra, says the *Encyclopaedia Britannica,* was a nine headed monster. As soon as one of its heads was cut off, two grew in its place. That is a superb description of music bibliography. In a Greek legend, Hydra was finally slain by Hercules with the help of Iolaus. In solving the awesome problems of music bibliography, we need a Hercules in the form of a computer and an Iolaus in the form of a widespread international cooperation by musicians, teachers, librarians and scholars. The bibliography of music is concerned with two major divisions: 1. literature about music and 2. music itself (including not only scores and parts, but thematic indexes and concordances, tapes and discs, etc.; this second division has bibliographical problems peculiar to itself because it deals with a non-verbal language). I will discuss computer applications to both divisions in turn.

First on literature about music. There is no difference in the methods of bibliographic control of books and articles about music from those of any other field. In music as in virtually all other disciplines we are in the midst of a very serious information crisis. It is a fact, for example, that the number of scholarly periodicals in all fields, music included, doubles every fifteen years and increases tenfold every fifty years. This means that there will be almost a thousand scholarly journals in music by the year 2015. Furthermore, if a given specialized area in research attracts a handful of scholars today, it will have fifty in a few years and hundreds in a few decades. Unless something is done about it, keeping abreast of one's discipline or even a little corner of one's discipline, will become an insurmountable task, and the resultant search fatigue and communication difficulties will become monstrous. The computer seems to be the only answer

11

although it must be emphasized that automation offers no pie in the bibliographical sky, and that every forward step in information retrieval has been hard fought and extremely costly of time and funds. In some areas there have been impressive developments: The *Index Medicus*, for example, is making important strides in controlling the world's medical literature. In the legal profession decisional law in some states is being stored, indexed and retrieved with computer help. Within twenty-four hours lawyers can get xeroxed copies of decisions pertinent to the case at hand saving themselves much wasteful search time. In government and industry, chemistry, biology, geography, and psychology, hundreds of thousands of articles and reports are abstracted annually and indexed with or without data processing equipment. Thus far, these control procedures are little known in music or in the humanities in general.

Modern techniques will inevitably change the very nature of bibliography and library science. Such studies as Linklider's slender volume, "Libraries of the Future", and the Council of Library Resources' study, "Automation and the Library of Congress," dramatically demonstrate the necessity, feasibility, and potential of automation. It is clear that automation's promise goes far beyond the mechanization of current functions. It includes revolutionary methods of document and information storage, retrieval and display, designed to make the library infinitely more active and effective in assisting the scholar and the student in their research activities.

The computer makes possible subject indexing to a depth humans would not dream of attempting. Why not fifteen or twenty subject headings for an important study rather than the usual, inadequate, two or three? Creative programming has developed new kinds of automatic indexing methods, e.g., KWIC, KWOC, WADEX, etc., that preserve man-hours and simplify retrieval. With respect to concordances, there are few scholarly techniques more appropriate for computer application. The num-

ber of excellent computer-assisted literary concordances produced thus far is impressive. Musical concordances using basically similar programming procedures will soon follow suit. Musical
notation, however, requires coding into machine-usable symbols,
such as numbers and letters. Several workable codes or input
languages have been developed for this purpose. The use of such
codes for music makes possible, for example, the preparation of
thematic indexes classified in a multitude of ways, the automatic
transposition of all incipits to C major and c minor, the identification of anonymi and the discovery of works of double attribu-
tion. More on this later.

A major tool of modern bibliography is the abstract. In the
control of current scientific and scholarly literature there seems
to be a great crescendo of abstracting activity, with and without
an obbligato of computer-generated indexes. There are over
2,000 abstracting organizations in the world today with at least
500 in the United States. None, may I repeat, exists for music,
except for a quarterly guide recently established in Philadelphia
that is on a popular rather than a scholarly level. Abstracts are
also employed in a system developed by IBM called SDI, "Se-
lective Dissemination of Information," the object of which is to
get the right document to the right person as soon as possible.
The principle is simple: Key words in the document's abstract
are compared by computer to the key words in the user's "pro-
file"; when a "match" is turned up by the computer, a copy of
the abstract is sent to the client who then decides whether or not
he desires to see the complete document.

Another very useful device is the aperture card. A frame of
microfilm is placed in a "window" aperture of a special punch
card; this card can be key punched, duplicated, sorted and filed
by data processing equipment. The technique of the aperture
card may be combined with that of super-micro photography to
produce the following pleasant fantasy. Micro-photography can
reduce a page to the size of a pinhead; thus an entire score or

text volume, several hundred pages in length, can be reproduced photographically, greatly reduced, in a single aperture window; identifying code numbers and cataloguing data can be added by keypunching the information onto the left side of the same card. The cards can then be sorted and stored automatically. The user, seated before a television console many miles away, presses buttons to call forth the visual display of the library's computer-prepared catalogues. He then asks for the desired volume by dialing its identifying call number; the equipment locates the aperture card, transmits its image electronically to the television console. The user never touches the aperture card. He never needs to hold a book. He merely looks at a screen and "flips" pages at will. If he wants to take a particular page away with him, he presses another button and out comes a xerox copy. This scholarly utopia does not exist at present. The technology for its realization, however, is fully developed and it, or something like it, will be available within not too many years.

A word about automatic scanning devices. It is now possible to read a number of type fonts by machine. This suggests the eventual possibility of computer generated indexes to machine produced abstracts of automatically scanned and stored documents! Furthermore, it is only the cost that keeps automatic scanning of music notation from becoming a reality. Four or five hundred thousand dollars is needed to develop a scanner that will be able to read notation and store it in the computer.

RILM: International Repertory of Music Literature

I would now like to discuss RILM, a specific plan to make use of data processing equipment for music documentation. RILM gets its title from the French version of its name, *Répertoire International de la Littérature Musicale*. RILM is an abstracted, computer-indexed bibliography of scholarly literature on music jointly sponsored by the International Musicological Society and the International Association of Music Libraries. It has been con-

14

ceived as the counterpart in music literature of the similarly sponsored, twelve year old, International Inventory of Musical Sources (RISM). Like RISM, it will be governed by an international commission. Unlike RISM, which is based in Europe where most of the earlier musical sources are to be found, RILM will have its international center in the United States where both the literature and the computers are available. In this country, the project is supported by the American Musicological Society, the Music Library Association and the American Council of Learned Societies.

RILM will have two principal publication series, one for current literature and the other for retrospective material. Current RILM will compile and publish abstracts and computer generated indexes of all scholarly writings on music published after January 1, 1967, including:

1. Periodicals (First Priority)
   A. Scholarly musicological periodicals
   B. Other musical periodicals (selected articles only)
   C. Non-musical periodicals (selected articles only)
2. Collective volumes
   A. Yearbooks
   B. Festschriften
   C. Congress reports
   D. Collection of essays, studies, etc.
3. Individual works
   A. Books
   B. Dissertations
   C. Monographs, pamphlets, essays, reports, introductions and Kritische Berichte to scholarly editions (Denkmäler and Gesamtausgaben).

All scholars are being requested to prepare abstracts, preferably although not necessarily, in English, for all of their writings published after January 1, 1967. Abstracts of periodical articles should be sent to the editor of the journal. The same holds true for yearbook articles. Abstracts for all other writings will be channeled through national RILM committees now being established or may be sent directly to the international RILM center at Queens College, Flushing, N. Y. 11367. All abstracts will bear the name of the abstractor and will be published in English with, ultimately, cross-indexing in other languages.

Retrospective RILM will ultimately compile and publish union periodical indexes by author, title, and where possible, key words for articles published prior to December 31, 1966. The computer will make massive cross-indexing feasible. The first order of business for the retrospective part of RILM will be the preparation of a Check List of Indexes to scholarly musical periodicals (published, manuscript, card files, etc.).

Cumulative indexes, automatically generated and printed, will be published regularly. Specialized bibliographies of all kinds with and without abstracts will be published individually. Scholars working on specific research projects will eventually be able to request a bibliographical search by the computer of the stored information and to receive an automatically printed out reply. Ultimately RILM should be self-supporting from the proceeds of its publications and from the fees from institutions and individuals requesting specialized information services.

It is hardly necessary to repeat that existing bibliographies of current literature in music, such as the *Bibliographie des Musikschriftums* and the *Music Index* are years behind now and get further behind each day. Although RILM's mythical goal, total bibliographical control of scholarly information about music past and present, is only a dream, and although its potential hurdles, e.g.—international cooperation, financial support, multiplicity of languages, etc., are frightening to contemplate, it is clear that the time has come for action and it is increasingly obvious that electronic data processing plus international cooperation is the answer.

The need for an international solution to the documentation problem in music has not wanted for recognition. Vladimir Fedorov was concerned about it at the Lüneburg congress in 1950. Alexander Hyatt King amplified the discussion to include abstracts in the Paris congress in 1951.[2] In 1955, *Fontes Artis Musicae* published a *Communiqué du Secretariat* entitled "Musicological Index".[3] There the promising plan was dropped; several of its features will be found incorporated in the present project.

It should also be pointed out that a quarter of a century ago the American Council of Learned Societies sponsored the publication of a series of musicological abstracts entitled "A Bibliography of Periodical Literature in Musicology and Allied Fields assembled for the Committee on Musicology of the ACLS by D. H. Daugherty, Leonard Ellinwood, and Richard S. Hill." Only two volumes appeared: 1938-39 and 1939-40. In the second volume for example, 57 contributors examined 245 journals, including non-musical ones, in many languages. The roster of contributors of abstracts includes such names as: Otto E. Albrecht, Willi Apel, J. Murray Barbour, Hans T. David, Leonard Ellinwood, Glen Haydon, George Herzog, Ernst Krenek, Ernst C. Krohn, Arthur Mendel, and Leo Schrade. These volumes mark an admirable isolated attempt; the difficulty was that there was no way of getting at the information, which remained unindexed and hence irretrievable, except by reading through all of it. The computer can be programmed to perform these functions automatically for vast quantities of abstracts.

The immediate goal of RILM is the control of current periodi-

1. "Entente et organisation internationales pour le dépouillement des périodiques musicaux" in 2. *Weltkongress der Musikbibliotheken, Lüneburg, 1950, Kongressbericht,* pp. 49-52.

2. "International scheme for publishing summaries of articles in musical periodicals" in *Troisième congrès international des bibliothèques musicales,* Paris, 1951.

3. *Fontes* 1955 No. 2, pp. 97-103.

cal literature, starting with January 1, 1967; subsequently, current theses, books, Festschriften, annuals, etc., will be included. Cooperation will be sought with Florence Kretzschmar of the *Music Index* and with Wolfgang Schmieder of the *Bibliographie des Musikschriftums* in an effort to avoid duplication of effort.

The essential building block of current RILM is the abstract. Most directors of abstracting organizations seem to agree that in the long run the author prepared abstract is the best. It is at worst a document in itself, indicating what the author thinks he said. In the sciences, abstracts are often required before an article will be accepted for publication in a scholarly journal. This is not now the case in the humanities. The ACLS has advocated this procedure. If it could come to pass in music, a giant stride forward will have been taken. For RILM, when the author fails to provide an abstract, the journal or festschrift editor, scholars, librarians and graduate students will be invited to do so. In some of the smaller countries of Europe, the national library will be the natural clearing house for the abstracting process; librarians in at least three of these countries have already agreed to arrange for the abstracting work. There are a number of professors of musicology and of music library science who have agreed to supervise their graduate students in the preparation of abstracts. Obviously the field is so vast that extensive cooperation will be required if the RILM project is to succeed.

A word on the difficult question of language. A committee of the International Musicological Society has been working for several years on a seven language "polyglot dictionary" of musical terms. When this lexicon is completed its entire data may readily be stored in computer memory. It would then be possible, when requesting a bibliographic print-out on any given topic, to have the computer automatically search appropriate subject headings under all of its stored languages. This would avoid the complications of machine translation which bogs down in the semantic subtleties of word interrelationships.

In automatic processing, once the data is stored, a variety of indexing techniques and print-outs is possible; the RILM system is designed to be flexible and open ended, to anticipate the use of visual scanners and automatic abstracting techniques now under experimentation, and to provide for interdisciplinary linkage. In this connection, the American Council of Learned Societies has called on journal editors and other representatives of its constituent societies to plan for a gigantic interdisciplinary bibliographical center to control current humanistic literature. The center will have the benefit of a staff of programmers who will concentrate on such problems as index generation, auto-abstracting, and retrieval techniques for limitless quantities of data in many disciplines. RILM has been designated as one of the two pilot projects of this ACLS Bibliographic Control Center.

I should like now to turn to the other major area of music bibliography—music itself. The problem here is very different from that of conventional bibliography because music is not an alphanumeric language and its proper classification and identification often require reference to music notation. One of the most pressing needs in music bibliography today is for a simple code system that can be readily learned and internationally accepted. The several reasons for this have already been discussed in an earlier paper on the subject.[1] One point, however, needs restating here: No matter how complete and precise the cataloguing, *positive identification of a large percentage of musical sources is not possible without including musical incipits* (ten or twelve notes suffice); and since conventional notation is too time

1. Barry S. Brook and Murray Gould, "Notating Music with Ordinary Typewriter Characters (A Plaine and Easie Code System for Musicke)" in *Fontes Artis Musicae* XI/3 (1964) 142-155. The present discussion of the "Simplified Plaine and Easie Code" is taken from the author's proposal for international adoption presented at the Congress of the International Association of Music Libraries in Dijon, July 3, 1965 and later published in its Proceedings in *Fontes* XII/2-3 (1965) 156-160.

consuming to write down, too costly to reproduce, and not suitable for electronic data processing, these incipits must be given in some coded form using ordinary typewriter or key punch characters. Thus far, none of the many code systems already in existence has succeeded in gaining widespread international acceptance. It is greatly to be deplored that RISM did not officially agree upon, and decide to use, *some* workable incipit code a dozen years ago. The Simplified Code described below is proposed in an effort to remedy the situation as much as it is possible to do so.

Even in the case of printed music, where title page data can be very helpful, identification is rarely certain:—the identical piece may be published with different opus numbers, under several different composers' names and by many different publishers. Thus, ten different-looking catalogue entries may all refer to the same work. If there exists a thematic catalogue of the composer's works, reference to the appropriate catalogue number would do the identification job, but too many composers lack adequate thematic indices of their works. It is said that it is now too late to add thematic incipits to the catalogue descriptions of printed sources already collected in the Kassel central office of RISM. Nevertheless, it is the personal opinion of the author, that, even at this late date if it is at all possible, the wisest course would be to attempt to do precisely that; that is, to add coded musical incipits to catalogue descriptions of all printed works or at least to those not otherwise positively identified. Even though this may add years to the publication date of the first alphabetic volumes of RISM and require great additional expenditure of time and effort, it would be well worth it.

Perhaps the most serious difficulty lies in the field of 17th- and 18th-century manuscript music, the sources for which outnumber prints by approximately 10 to 1. It is hardly conceivable that this vast body of musical source materials, which includes many anonymi and works of doubtful parentage, can be properly catalogued without some form of incipit code. This is precisely what RISM faces today. The problem is so acute for manuscript music because even the usual identifying title page paraphernalia (publisher's name, city, opus number, etc.) appearing with printed music is usually absent. When there is an accompanying vocal text precise identification is often possible, but for instrumental music one may be totally lost without the incipit. A composer may have written a *dozen* trio sonatas in D major, for example, and no conventional cataloguing will distinguish one from the other; only the incipit will do this.

Whatever may be the situation for printed materials, it is earnestly to be hoped that it is not too late to add incipits to RISM's inventory of manuscript sources. Unless RISM finds some method of achieving positive identification of manuscripts, a vast amount of labor will be expended to achieve a fundamentally inadequate result.

The Simplified Plaine and Easie Code

The original version of "Notating Music with Ordinary Typewriter Characters: A Plaine and Easie Code System for Musicke" which appeared with valuable commentaries by Jan LaRue, Ingmar Bengtsson, Nanie Bridgman, Rita Benton, and Paule Chaillon-Guiomar *(Fontes,* XI, pp. 155-159) engendered a good deal of experimentation and discussion. It soon became apparent that modifications would be necessary to make the code more usable on an international basis and the present version incorporates the suggestions of many interested colleagues. The basic principle for using the simplified "Plaine and Easie" code in cataloguing remains the same: after the cataloguer has taken down the usual information from the title page he simply adds a coded incipit taken from the first page of music. Using the simplified code requires only a few additional seconds. Supplementary symbols found in the original version of "Plaine and Easie" can be added *ad libitum,* but for ordinary purposes the simplified

21

version is all that is required. Examples will be found below. In a few cases two symbols are listed, one, in lower case, more suitable for typewriter use, and the other, in capitals, for use on the key punch.

Part I (Preliminary Data):

Tempo, key signature, and *metre* are given first and in parentheses. Abbreviations are avoided in the interest of clarity. When either tempo, key signature, or metre is absent, this is indicated by a triple blank space, separated by commas, for example: (Adagio, , 4/4) indicating that there are no sharps or flats in the signature.

Tempo: written out fully; metronome marking, if present, is added immediately afterward. MM 2 = 120 (half note equals 120) or MM 16 = 240 (sixteenth note = 240).

Key signature (tonalité, Tonart): A sharp (# or X) or flat (b or Y) followed by the letter names of the sharps or flats as they appear, e.g. #FCG. *Optional:* In the case of minor keys and partial or unusual signatures, an additional descriptive word or symbol (e.g. minor, serial) *may* be added; this is the only part of the code where interpretation may be possible. An exclamation point (!) indicates an incomplete or an unusual signature (e.g. in Baroque music or in Bartók).

Metre (mesure, Taktart): Given exactly as indicated in the music, without abbreviations, for example: 3/4, 2/2, 2, C, ₵, 3, O, etc. [*Optional:* Preceding the parentheses the *movement number, instrument or voice,* and *clef* may be indicated. *Movement number* is given in Roman numerals, but only when *not* the first movement. *Instrument or voice:* Usually the principal uppermost voice is employed for the incipit and it need *not* be named; exceptions *should* be mentioned here. When two or more parts are given, they appear one above the other. *Clef:* Only when *not* treble, e.g. C-3 clef for viola (C clef on third line).]

22

Thus, for the third movement of Beethoven's Fifth Symphony, Part I of the incipit, including optional information before the parentheses, would read:

III, cello, F-4 clef (Allegro, bBEAminor, 3/4). Meaning:

Third movement, incipit from cello, F clef on the fourth line; Allegro, three flats—key of C minor, 3/4 metre.

Part II (The Notes):

In the writing out of the notes, there are essentially only two variables: *duration* and *pitch*. It is the author's firm belief that a successful code must include both variables so that it can be readily recognized as music and can be completely retranslated back to conventional notation without any loss.

Duration: The duration of notes or rests is given, as in the original version, by the use of numbers. These numbers appear *before* pitch letters or rests and remain in effect without being restated until cancelled by a different duration number or by the small letter "g" indicating a grace note.

1	Whole-note or rest
2	Half-note or rest
4	Quarter-note, etc.
8	Eighth-note
6	Sixteenth-note
3	Thirty-second note
5	Sixty-fourth note
7	One-hundred-and-twenty-eighth-note
9	Breve
0	Longa

Dotted notes are indicated as in conventional notation, by a period following the duration number. Thus: 2.C 4D = dotted half-note C followed by quarter-note D.

Rests are indicated by a dash " — ".

Ties are indicated by an underline " _ ".

Pitches (hauteurs, Tonhöhe) are indicated by the capital letters A B C D E F G. Accidentals # or X, ## or XX, b or Y, bb or YY, n or N (natural) precede the pitch letters exactly as in conventional music. (Alternates for #, b, n, i.e. X, Y, N, are for use on key punch.)

Octave Placement or Register: This represents a major change from the original version which employed a complicated "referential" system of octave placement. The present octave placement method is an "absolute" system, given as an alternate in the original paper.[1]

Example 1

The comma or apostrophe octave symbols remain in effect without being restated until another octave symbol is introduced. Octave symbols precede duration numbers. Thus, in the same example of Beethoven's Fifth Symphony, the incipit would be fully encoded as follows:

Example 2

(Allegro, bBEAminor, 3/4) ,,4G /,C E G /'2C 4E /2D ,4#F /2.G_ /G/

This system of octave symbols is consistent with that of duration numbers, both remaining in effect until cancelled. Both have the added virtue of being repeatable, in case any doubt exists, without affecting the result in any way. Thus, in 4/4 metre: 2C 4EG / GE 2C / (half-note, quarter, quarter/ quarter, quarter, half/) means the same thing as: 2C 4EG / 4G 4E 2C/. In similar fashion, the pitches of Frère Jacques would be written thus in

1. Fontes XI/3 [1964] p. 146.

24

C major: 'CDEC / CDEC / EFG; this would be identical to: CDEC / 'CDEC / 'EFG.

To take another familiar example, the incipit of Mozart's G minor Symphony falls within a single octave therefore only a single octave symbol is required.

Example 3

(Molto allegro, bBEminor, ¢) 2- 4- "8ED / 4D 8ED 4D 8ED / 4D B

Here is an example of a complete catalogue card from the Queens College Music Library in which, by the simple addition of a one line-incipit, which took the cataloguer exactly thirty additional seconds to complete, a little known Sammartini overture is positively identified.

The first violin incipit in conventional notation (with incomplete signature) appears as follows:

Example 4

The complete catalogue card, with coded incipit included, appears thus:

M	Sammartini, Giovanni Battista, 1701-1775
61	[Overture. Strings. C minor]
S18	Overture.
BL24	
	score (11p.) 27 x 35 cm.

Xerox reproduction of modern copyist's score of 18th cent. manuscript parts Blancheton 24. ["before 1742", B. Churgin.]

(Allegro, bBEminor!, 3/4) "4.C 6— 'C8.E6G/"4C C C/
1. Overtures—Full score.

Additional Symbols:

The more useful symbols from the original paper are given here in order to facilitate use of the Simplified Code without having to refer back to the previous version:

_ (underline) or + (plus)	Tie: a single underline with no character above it or a plus sign.
/	Bar line.
/ /	Double bar line.
( )	Fermata when enclosing single pitch (letter) or rest; e.g. 2(D) = fermata over half note D; 4D (−) = fermata over quarter-note rest.
( )	Unusual rhythmic grouping such as triplets, quintuplets, etc., are enclosed in parentheses. Thus: (8CDE) means triplet eighth-notes CDE.
(7)	Unusual rhythmic grouping clarified by the addition of the number usually superimposed in conventional notation just before the closed parentheses.
(( ))	Double parentheses enclose changes in tempo, key signature, or metre that occur in the course of a piece.
/ − /	Full measure rest.
/ −3 /	Three measures rest.
/ : /	Repeat preceding measure.
/ :2 /	Repeat two preceding measures.
/ /: :/ /	Repeat signs as in conventional notation.
t or T	Trill; precedes pitch letter: t8D = trill eighth-note D.

w or W	Tremolo; precedes pitch letter: w8D = tremolo eighth-note D.
s or S	Turn, mordent and all embellishments that are indicated by a sign rather than a specific pitch designation like the grace note.
g or Q	Grace note; also used for cue sized notes.
! or *	Exclamation point or asterisk; indication of incomplete or unusual key signature.

Conclusion:

The Simplified Plaine and Easie Code has eliminated several of the difficulties of the earlier version. It is now being successfully employed for a number of bibliographic and analytical projects here and abroad. In this country, Jan La Rue is using it somewhat modified, for his invaluable union catalogues of 18th century symphonies and concertos. Murray Gould at Queens College has developed an adaptation for Gregorian Chant; several scholars have been applying it to the indexing of ethnomusicological sources; others are using it for the establishment of thematic catalogues, e.g. Walter Gerboth and J. Dean Brown's computer-indexed thematic catalogue of the complete works of Ludwig Senfl; finally, George Logemann of New York University and Murray Gould have expanded the code into a complete language which can translate and store in a computer entire compositions, including harmony, dynamics, phrasing, etc., permitting complicated analyses of style and structure.

It is hoped that the Simplified Plaine and Easie Code may be found helpful to many other scholars and librarians, and especially to RISM in its efforts to cope with its enormous task of cataloguing the vast ocean of manuscript sources before 1800.

Computer-Implemented Analysis of Musical Structure

by
Allen Forte

"Would you tell me, please, which way I ought to go from here?"
"That depends a good deal on where you want to go," said the Cat.
"I don't much care where—" said Alice.
"Then it doesn't matter which way you go," said the Cat.
"—so long as I get *somewhere*," Alice added as an explanation.
"Oh, you're sure to do that," said the Cat, "if you only walk long enough."

The evident increase of interest in the use of the computer in music research does not come as a surprise. Nor are some unfortunate aspects of this pioneer phase unexpected. The "gee whiz" syndrome which is now very much in the foreground is certain to become less common, and emphasis will be placed, properly so, in the quality of research work and on its relevance to important problems. Two necessary and interrelated processes will help to assure intelligent use of computing machines in music: high-level education and the dissemination of information. This suggests that we must be concerned, even at this early stage, with criteria, lest we offend both technology and art. In the course of the discussion I will indicate what I believe to be important guides.

The sequence of topics is as follows: (1) Some comments on computer applications in non-scientific fields; (2) Reasons for using the computer for analysis; (3) Some computer problems relevant to music research; (4) Basic requirements on projects in structural analysis; (5) Sketch of one part of my present work; (6) Concluding remarks.

Before proceeding to the main part of the paper it may be well to explain the term "computer-implemented", which is used in the title. This term means that the computer is programmed

31

in such a way that it does the largest part of the work for the researcher. Computer-implemented studies therefore are distinct from what one might call "computer-aided" studies, in which the role of the machine is not predominant—as when the machine is used in the solution of a subproblem.

On Computer Applications in Non-Scientific Fields

In a very short time we have changed our view of the computer as a giant calculator in the service of commerce and the sciences to one which takes into account the diverse applications that have been made in many non-scientific fields. To some of us, even in such recondite fields as music theory, access to an advanced computer system is both familiar and necessary. Yet it is clear that we are still in a pioneer stage, and it may be wise to consider some of the difficulties experienced at that stage in other non-scientific fields, in the hope that we will be better prepared to meet these if they arise.

Among the difficulties commonly encountered in non-scientific computer research the following is prominent. After an initial phase of progress it is discovered that the research task was either so routine as to be insignificant or not sufficiently well-defined to lead to a machine-implemented solution. In part this is a consequence of the lack of precedents for the use of the computer in the particular field. It may also indicate that the traditional methodology of the discipline is inadequate. Closely associated with this difficulty is the lack of appropriate mathematics or logic, conceptual apparatus, means of representing data, and techniques of validating. It may be that these are all available, yet not designed in such a way that they are accessible to computer programming. Two courses of action are open to the researcher who finds himself in this unhappy circumstance: discreet withdrawal or more work.

At a more immediate and practical level, there is the problem of obtaining qualified assistants. Persons well versed in data-processing methods (professional computer people) may be ignorant of the field of application. One would not wish to delegate responsibility for complex work deeply involved in the detail of a subject-area. For this reason alone the researcher who wishes to make extensive use of the machine for non-trivial work must himself be a competent programmer. Even if he does not do all the programming, he can hardly understand the research work, let alone supervise it, if he has not had intensive programming experience.

Some Reasons for Using the Computer for Analysis

The first reason often given for using the computer is that it can process a large quantity of data very rapidly. This reason is good, but it does not cover the situation adequately. (Moreover, it tends to emphasize the routine, book-keeping aspects of computer applications—and these are unworthy of the attention of the serious researcher in any field.) A better reason follows from the property of great speed: The computer can be programmed to deal with complex structures—such as a musical composition —very rapidly. This means that programs can be written, tested, and modified within a short time-span, thus permitting the researcher to experiment with a large range of possibilities. I do not overlook the fact, however, that it may require many hours of careful work to create a stock of basic programs before such experimentation can begin.

A second reason for using the computer derives from the requirements of completeness and precision that form the basis of every computer program. For the researcher who is concerned about reliability and who needs to know the process by which his results are obtained, and to know this at every phase, the computer affords a facility unmatched by any other device. The design of an algorithm, the formulation of a decision-structure to solve a problem, the careful checking out of a malfunctioning program—all these activities provide clarifications and insights which would be difficult, perhaps impossible, to obtain otherwise.

Some Computer Problems Relevant to Music Research

There is ample evidence in a number of fields that so-called brute-force methods are ineffectual in the solution of complex problems. In particular, attempts to prove theorems by long heuristic programs or to construct translations by primitive dictionary look-up have failed. From the standpoint of the programmer, complex processes are complex. This fact is well known to workers in the field of artificial intelligence. The popular view of the computer as a question-answering device is very quickly abandoned by the novice programmer. When designing an algorithm one does not ask questions, except in the metaphorical sense.

A second and more specific problem-area is that of techniques for representing output. Typically, the researcher has a data-set of some kind which he wishes to have transformed in some way by the execution of a program. It may be that his data-set has already undergone a transformation. For example, he may have decided to omit certain characteristics or to assign priorities of some kind before processing begins. After his program has been executed he may happily gather up his results, only to discover that they are exceedingly difficult to read or that they do not inform him. This reflects the operation of certain familiar constraints under which the computer user works. It should be said here that much work is being done by professional computer people to alleviate these difficulties and that the present limitations probably will be regarded as primitive within a few years. Even the general availability of a greatly enlarged character-set will be a significant advance. More dramatic developments, particularly optical displays, will offer many possibilities not now available. The fundamental problem of representation, however,

34

will remain, for the researcher will have to make basic decisions which are intimately bound up with his work. Further on I will approach this point from a different direction.

Limitations upon the size of computer memories present very basic difficulties to the researcher. It is quite easy for a program to use the 32,000 words of memory available in one of the most commonly used large computers. Current remedies include the use of secondary storage, especially disk storage, with appropriate software to permit rapid access and to allow chaining of programs. At another level, the programming language itself may provide dynamic storage, in which case the programmer may have available three or four times the theoretical memory capacity. The long-range solution is said to be the development of inexpensive, large associative memory. At present, however, limited storage capacity is a reality which the researcher must be prepared to meet. It would not be advisable, for example, to plan a program to count all the major triads in the Bach Cantatas—at least not to be done in a single run. And it is probably not advisable to do this anyway, for other reasons!

The selection of a programming language should be discussed, since it is of prime importance to any computer project. Only certain essentials can be reviewed here. Let us consider, first, the three major classes of problem-oriented, high-level computer languages now available.

(1) Algebraic languages

These languages are intended primarily for scientific work. Characteristically they have powerful arithmetic and can handle large numbers with ease. The fundamental data-structure is the array. Examples include FORTRAN, MAD, ALGOL.

(2) List-processing languages

These languages are designed for problems in logic. The fundamental data-structure is the linked-list. The power of this class of languages resides in its ability to manipulate complex structures, for example by searching a complex tree or by tracing intricate paths on a graph. The language LISP is an example.

(3) String-manipulating languages

Here the fundamental data-structure is the free string, a "one dimensional" sequence of characters. These languages excel in manipulating structures which can be represented, or which are most appropriately represented, as strings. An example is the language SNOBOL.

Now, the point of this is that there are various ways of representing, of "conceptualizing", structure by means of a programming language. When a researcher selects a language, therefore, his thought and procedures, his interpretation of output, his formulation of problems, and many other essential aspects of his work are subject to influence by the limitations and particular attributes of the language. Certain kinds of operations, such as the free scan, are natural to the SNOBOL language, whereas other operations—for example, the systematic search of a 3-dimensional array, which would be natural in FORTRAN, is not natural to SNOBOL.

The matter of special-purpose programming languages for music research should be mentioned here, since it will probably crop up regularly in the future. Should such languages be designed and used? In my opinion, the answer is no, for the following reasons. First, there is the question of availability. There is no assurance that such a language would be implemented, and more importantly, be maintained, at computer installations. Consequently, provincialism would be encouraged. Second, who is to make the basic decisions regarding data-structures? Who is to decide upon the kinds of operations in the language? There has not yet been enough work done to assure that any such decisions would meet general needs. The general-purpose languages now available almost everywhere (including those listed above) offer powerful resources which have not yet been tapped, and have the additional advantage that they are adequately documented and maintained at a great many university computer installations.

At a more intensive and advanced stage we can expect certain other important questions to arise. How much is the researcher willing to delegate to the machine? How are the familiar terms "experience" and "intuition" to be interpreted in the context of computer work? These questions are especially pressing in the case of humanities research, and it is evident that they cause concern to many serious professional persons. A provisional answer to many such questions is that we do not yet know how far we can go. The intellectual challenges and the possibility of achieving results unobtainable otherwise will continue to attract researchers. As one consequence, the number of easily solved problems will diminish rapidly, while new discoveries will suggest new and more interesting problems—much as happens now in the sciences. Those members of the academic community who traffic in the routine do have cause for concern, although perhaps not in the immediate future. Others—and this group will unquestionably include a large proportion of the younger scholars—will have open to them a new and exciting universe for significant research.

Some Requirements on Analysis Projects

Before setting forth what I regard as some of the basic requirements on analysis, I would like to make some observations. First, a serious analysis project is a difficult matter. The computer, despite its extraordinary speed, does not provide fast answers. Second, the use of the computer does not validate an analysis. Results can be wrong. The program may contain a flaw which does not show up until after having been executed a number of times. Third, a particular problem might be solved more efficiently by hand. If one wished to study the components of a process, however, even if that process could be carried out easily by hand, a

37

program would obviously be in order. Fourth, there is no justification for a computer-implementation of a poor analytic method. What does it mean to write a program that labels chords in the manner of Riemann? It would be comforting to believe that all such procedures will be short-lived in this pioneer stage of research.

Milton Babbitt has said: "The problem of analysis, of course, is that of significance, not of identification." This felicitous comment provides a point of departure for the somewhat condensed list of requirements on analysis projects given below.

(1) An analysis project will necessarily be concerned with elements of some kind. It cannot, however, be limited to the construction of uninterpreted lists of those elements, but must extend to consideration of the relations between them.

(2) It must recognize that relations may exist at more than one stratum. The factor of "depth" must, correspondingly, be made explicit.

(3) It must develop effective tools for dealing with levels of relations—for example, adequate means of representing them symbolically.

The conditions for meeting these requirements are readily available in the data-processing environment and it is to be hoped that designers of research projects will take advantage of the opportunity to discard some of the outworn apparatus of music theory which has consistently inhibited general acceptance of sound basic method in analysis.

Sketch of a Computer Project

I will now outline a basic part of the computer project which I have been carrying out during recent months.* The long-range goal of the project is to formulate a structural description of the class of compositions commonly called "atonal". Specifically, this

*A detailed description of this work is scheduled for publication in a Project MAC Technical Report late in 1966.

includes the post-tonal, pre-12-tone works of Schoenberg, Berg, Webern, and several other composers—among them, Bartok and Ives. A set of programs written in the MAD programming language performs certain higher-level operations on a data-set representing event-configurations extracted from a complete score. These operations include the determination of similarities and differences, the interpretation of those with respect to characteristics of the environments in which they occur, and the design of a structural model in terms of set-complex theory. In addition, a method of accumulating and retrieving historical and other comments in natural language has been devised. As a result, each time the programs are executed comments are added to the list and comments are printed out. This appears to be a very useful tool for the analyst since it gives him a flexible and informal view of some aspects of the information being processed and may suggest areas of particular interest which should be examined more closely. I turn now to the main features of part of the project: a system of score-reading, believed to be the first of its kind.

The score-reading system accepts as input a free string of code representing music notation. The input language from which the code is drawn was designed by Stefan Bauer-Mengelberg in connection with a project to print scores automatically. This language has special advantages: (1) It is isomorphic to music notation; (2) the logical structure of the language and its mnemonics render it easy to learn and to read; (3) the language is especially suited to the analysis of music, since it contains no prior decisions with respect to structure, other than those which one would find in the score. That is to say, it is non-interpretive. As one consequence of this property, the responsibilities of the encoder are minimal. He need make no decisions regarding, for example, the "line" a particular note belongs to. (4) The language is complete: Any character sequence found in a conventional score can be represented.

The basic purpose of the score-reading system is to structure, by means of a parsing process, the raw data represented in the input string. By parsing is meant the extraction of all and only those representatives of certain defined classes of event-configurations. One such fundamental class, for example, is called the class of primary segments, a class which contains all segments set off by rests in individual instrument parts. Each event-configuration is associated with a set of reference-points in a numerical representation of a time-continuum. The latter feature makes it possible to view the structured data as a set of temporal relations: Any event, from the atomic level to the level of extended segments, can be compared to any other with respect to their positions in time. Thus, the program not only permits the specification of characteristics of local contexts but also affords the possibility of examining relations between contexts in the time dimension.

At present the system comprises three linked programs written in the programming language SNOBOL3. The initial sequence of operations is as follows:

(1) The data file is read.

(2) The data file is scanned for certain kinds of encoding errors.

(3) A search is made for the complete character string corresponding to each instrumental part.

(4) For each "time-code" in the input language a position-value (a number) is computed.

(5) All members of the class of primary segments are found and for each of these certain categories of information are represented in a fixed format called an output form.

The programs then parse for five other classes of event-configurations, deleting character-classes in the input string and duplicate segments in accord with a set of rules representing the basic programming logic.

40

Some elementary features of the system require further comment. The input data file of course remains intact. No information is lost from it and it is always available for processing again. Theoretically, there is no limit to the number of structural characteristics which could be handled by the parsing process. At present, however, the system deals only with a limited number of these, and any information in the input language which is not relevant to the processor is either by-passed or deleted. This answers, I believe, the question of the value of "partial encoding". As Bauer-Mengelberg has pointed out, there is no valid reason for encoding a score in some incomplete fashion, when it is possible to have all the information available for scanning.

Because the basis of the parsing system is syntactic, in the sense that parsing operations are performed on formal structures in the input string, many extensions and refinements can be made without excessive difficulty. Further, the system is general. It is not constrained or determined in any way by the historical period from which the data file is drawn or by considerations of style. On the other hand, it may be possible to effect further refinements by taking into consideration particular details of structure. This could be done by extending the program to include more and more inductive features, in such a way that it would make necessary modifications of logic during processing. An extension of this kind would greatly increase the heuristic power of the system.

For the time being I am leaving open the question of whether this score-reading system simulates the work of the human analyst. Over the long range this question may, in fact, be irrelevant. For the present I can only say that the system works well, that it does many interesting and sometimes quite unexpected things, and that although it operates at an elementary stage in the analytic hierarchy, the work which it does is not at all lacking in refinement and subtlety.

41

Concluding Remarks

Despite the rapid progress in computer technology the average user may still have to wait some time before he has access to an advanced system. By an advanced system I mean particularly a system which is designed for time-sharing, such as the extensive experimental facility of Project MAC at M.I.T. In a time-sharing situation the user communicates with the computer via remote terminal (either a teletype machine or a suitably modified typewriter). Under good operating conditions response time is so brief that he has the happy illusion that he is the sole user of the machine, while in reality there may be as many as 30 other users. All programs and data files are stored on a disk and punched cards are used only for back-up in case of catastrophe. Many systems subroutines are available to the user merely by typing a command at his terminal.

Perhaps the most significant result of access to a system of this kind is that it permits the user to move rapidly between stages of experimentation and formalization; two processes which are essential to high-level research directed toward the development of empirical theories. When such systems become more widely available and when qualified persons gain sufficient experience to be able to use them with facility we can anticipate a marked impact on music research. Meanwhile, we can certainly continue to learn from our own work and from other work in progress and to prepare the way for sensible and fruitful use of the computer toward the solution of significant problems.

Computers and the Study of Musical Style

by
Gerald Lefkoff

In many musical studies a model of a musical composition is used. The model is examined and information extracted, information which is then processed according to the requirements of the study. Such operations can be executed with a computer. The ensuing discussion will be concerned with computer-residing musical models and their use in the study of style. The term style is here used in reference to specifications of populations of musical specimens. This is distinct from structural-analysis in which an individual composition is studied as an entity. Some typical computer-implemented style-study procedures will be presented. This is not intended to be an exhaustive presentation of such procedures but rather suggestive of the possibilities for the use of automated data-processing techniques for style-study. This discussion will be related to a group of programs called MUSTUD which I have been developing for the study of computer-residing, score-derived musical models.

In many studies it is unnecessary and impractical to examine a real musical object as it sounds in performance. It is unnecessary since the sought information is available elsewhere, and impractical since information retrieval in real time is difficult and expensive. All that is needed is a model which contains the information required by the particular study. The musical score has been a standard model for the study of music. It is rich in information which is presented in a form with which there is widespread familiarity, and many such models are readily available. Models other than the score can of course also be useful.

A model which is constructed within a computer can be studied efficiently and accurately. Such models may be designed for special or general use. A special purpose model need contain no information that is superfluous to the study for which it is designed and it may therefore be a simple structure which is easily constructed and studied. Lacking a body of general purpose models with associated utility routines, special purpose models may be expedient for some studies. While the requirements of a study are formulated prior to the construction of the special purpose model, the general purpose model precedes a study and limits it. When a model is used, the problem of the study is ultimately formulated in terms of the model rather than the real object. A collection of existing general purpose models tends therefore to channel scholarship and to orientate the mode of scholarly thought. This limitation, which is not in itself undesirable, is counter-balanced by the convenience of implementing studies with pre-existent models and associated apparatus.

Two major sources from which information may be derived for constructing computer residing, general purpose models of music, are musical scores and musical performances. It may be expected that both sources will be tapped and that the structure and use of the score derived and sound derived model will be rather different. This discussion will be limited to general purpose score derived models of music.

The score derived model need not, and in most cases will not contain all the information that resides in the score itself. Such things as pagination, watermarks, type peculiarities, and even dynamics and fingerings, may be excluded from the computer model. The design of the computer model will depend upon the information that it is to contain as well as computer requirements, requirements such as coding, efficiency of constructing and searching the model, and compactness; and many designs may be satisfactory. The model used in MUSTUD will be described in the following section as an example of one such design.

MUSTUD is written in FORTRAN and the structure of the model exploits FORTRAN's facility for handling arrays. The various kinds of information contained in the score are separated

46

and stored in independent arrays which are cross referenced to a time index. The time index is a one dimensional array with the subscript indicating the ordinal location of the event and the stored value indicating the location in continuous time measured in quarter notes. The pitches are represented in a two dimensional array with each voice assigned a location in the array. The values stored in one column indicate the ordinal location of the pitch event referencing the time index array, and the values stored in the corresponding row of another column represent the concert pitches. Other arrays arranged in the two dimensional manner of the pitch array, may be used to list vocal text, figured bass symbols, dynamics and articulations, and editorial comments. After the time indexed arrays are constructed, they are stored on a library tape along with information which is not time indexed, information such as library cataloguing designations, bibliographical citations, editorial comments and notation description which cannot be reconstructed from the time indexed section of the model. A feature of this procedure which should be noted is that the library storage tape does not contain a description of the score in the form of the input language. Instead the input is transformed and stored as a computer-oriented musical model. This model may be retrieved for study at any time.

The program in MUSTUD which constructs and stores the musical model is called MUMODL. The input for the MUMODL program is a transcription of the printed musical score the preparation of which requires little interpretation of the score itself. This input is in two parts. A sample of the first part is shown in example 1. Some of this input is not used to construct the model itself and is placed directly upon a library tape. The variables defined under PARTS are used to determine the transposition addend required for the calculation of the concert pitches. The variables defined under METER are used in routines which perform conversions between the time index of the model and the measures and beats of the printed score.

47

```
CATALOGUE DESIGNATION/WVUIOT
COMPOSER/JOHN FICTITIOUS
TITLE/VARIATIONS ON AN UNKNOWN TUNE
SOURCE/COMPLETE WORKS OF JOHN FICTITIOUS,NEW YORK,ZXY PRESS,1965
COMMENT/THIS IS A SIMULATED COMPOSITION TO TEST THE MUMODL PROGRAM AND MUST OD R
RETRIEVAL ROUTINES
TEMPI/ADAGIO,ALLEGRO(MEASURE 37),PRESTO(MEASURE 110)
METER/3-4,4-4(MEASURE 37),6-8(MEASURE 110)
PARTS/1,SOPRANO,2,VIOLIN,3,OBOE-ENGLISH HORN(MEASURE 63)-OBOE(MEASURE 75),4,CLA
RINET IN B FLAT,5,HORN IN F,6,CELLO,7,BASS VIOLIN
```

Example 1

48

The second and main part of the input is prepared on a special coding sheet which is shown in example 2. Example 3 shows the symbols which represent the position of the notes on the staff and their rhythmic value and accidentals.

Example 2

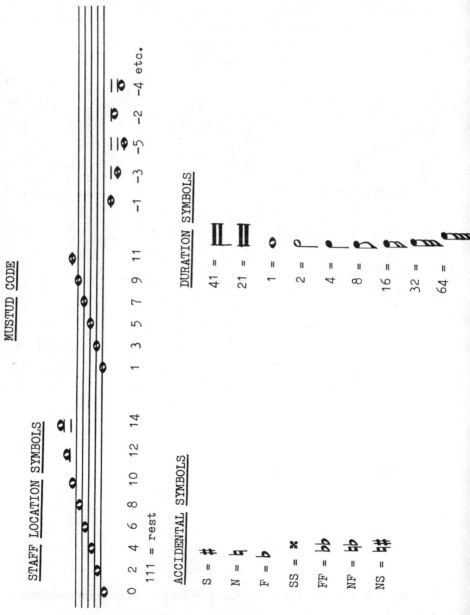

Example 3

50

A symbol for the key signature is entered in columns 31-32 on the card for the note before which it first appears. The clef name is entered in columns 25-30 on the card for the note before which it first appears. Symbols for the location of the notes on the staff (see example 3, STAFF LOCATION) are entered in columns 7-9 and the symbols for accidentals (see example 3, ACCIDENTAL SYMBOLS) are entered in columns 10-11. The concert pitch of each note is calculated using the transposition addend which is picked up from the PART designation in the first input section, the clef and key signature symbols, the staff location value, the accidental symbols, and a routine which determines if an accidental appearing earlier in the measure is applicable.

Symbols for the rhythmic values of the notes (see example 3, DURATION SYMBOLS) are entered in columns 13-14. These symbols may be omitted when they would be identical with the preceding symbol. A period or two is placed in the next field if the note has a dot or a double dot. A "T" is placed in column 12 when a note is tied to the preceding note. The proportional effect of duplets, triplets, quintuplets, etc., are represented by two digits in columns 17-18, which indicate the ratio of the new duration to the old. Thus 32 indicates that three notes occupy the place of two and 74 indicates that seven notes occupy the place of four, etc. This ratio applies until cancelled by a new ratio symbol. The duration of the note is calculate using the symbols for the duration, dot, ties and proportion. The measure number may be optionally entered in columns 21-23 to verify the accuracy of the rhythmic transcription. When there is an up beat an entry of measure number 1 is used to show the beginning of the first full bar. An integer may be entered in column 20 to indicate a number of repetitions of a card. Column 19 is used to indicate a continuation of the preceding card extending any field to the next card. The continue column is also used to indicate that a note begins simultaneously with the note previously entered. This is necessary for encoding keyboard scores. First and second

51

endings and repeat and decapo signs are entered in column 45. Text for singing and figured bass symbols may be entered in their fields and symbols for dynamics and articulations recorded in the columns 46-55.

Once a model of music is available, information can be extracted from it. If the model is a printed score and is visually studied, the examiner may begin with general specifications of the sought information; specifications which may be redefined as the score is examined. These specifications may be subjective or never explicitly stated. Furthermore the examiner may convert the visual model into sound, and extract some information from the musical object itself rather than from the model. Now to extract information from a model of music which resides within a computer, it is necessary to formulate precise, objective specifications of the sought information prior to the computer examination of the model. The formulation of such specification statements is a major theoretical task, and the need for such statements in computer-implemented studies enforces a discipline which may have a profound effect upon the mode of theoretical thinking.

A model of a composition may be thought of as the residence of various kinds of structures. Some of these sub-structures are often the formal object of a style study. The model of a sub-structure is of course a segment of the model of the composition. The initial processing then requires the extraction of model segments. The information contained in the model segment may vary in kind, order and quantity. For example it may represent two pitches, or an unordered pitch class set, or a series of concert pitches with associated durations, or a series of adjacent simultaneous pitches. To extract a model segment from the parent model it must be found by some locating criteria. The locating criteria may indicate only where the sought information is stored or it may also require a test of the stored information. If, for example, the sought segment is a set of concert pitches which occur simultaneously, the time index may be used to locate the pitches which are extracted without examination. However if a triad is sought in a structure where arpeggiation and non-chord tones occur, a series of adjacent simultaneous pitch sets may be examined to discover a triadic subset and its temporal range.

Once extracted, model segments may be processed independently of the parent model. They may be transformed, classified, tagged, sorted, counted and statistically processed. These procedures can be combined in many ways to satisfy the requirements of unique studies. A description of several typical procedures will follow to demonstrate some applications of information processing to music model segments.

A model segment may be transformed into a standard form to achieve some level of classification. In example 4 there is an illustration of some transformations performed upon a series of pitches.

Line 1 contains a series of pitches as it appears in a printed score. The values in line 2 correspond to the concert pitches as they are represented in the computer model. This is the model segment which is extracted from the parent model for processing. In line 3 the model segment has been transposed by adding -57 to each value so that a standard form with the first value as zero is produced. The semitone values of line three are converted into diatonic interval values in line 4. Line 5 is a series of pitch classes with C equal to zero. The model segment is transformed in line 6 to a pitch difference series, and in line 7 to an interval class series. In line 8 it is transformed to a pitch class set in normal order and its interval vector is presented in line 9. Line 10 contains a contour classification employing a packed symbol. Each symbol represents a turn in the line. Positive values indicate high points and negative values low points. The integer part

53

1. (musical staff with notes)

2. 57 59 64 56 57 52 62 60 59

3. 0 2 7 -1 0 -5 5 3 2

4. 1 2 5 -2 1 -4 4 3 2

5. 9 11 4 8 9 4 2 0 11

6. 2 5 -8 1 -5 10 -2 -1

7. 2 5 4 1 7 10 10 11

8. 0 1 3 5 6 8

9. 1 4 3 2 4 1

10. 3.07 -4.08 5.01 -6.05 7.10 -9.3

Example 4

indicates the ordinal position of the turning point and the decimal part indicates the pitch difference of the adjacent turning points.

In the following section the design for a rather large process will be discussed. The purpose of this process is first to produce a complete list of melodic fragments from a group of compositions, with frequency distribution data for the fragments within each composition and second to compare the relative frequency of occurrence of each fragment in selected groups of compositions. The principal steps in the processes are as follows:

1. *EXTRACT* all model segments meeting segment specifications from selected compositions stored on MUMODL LIBRARY TAPE. (Segment specifications: successive pitches in a distinct voice, size X to Y.)
2. *TRANSFORM* each segment by transposition. T = negative value of first pitch in each series.
3. *TAG* each segment with source tag designating parent model.
4. *LIST* on tape for further processing, each tagged, transformed model segment.
5. *SORT* first on tag, then on model segment.
6. *COUNT* frequency of each model segment with like tag. *CALCULATE* relative frequency of each segment in its segment class (classified by size).
7. *LIST* on tape for further processing and *PRINT* for examination: source tag, frequency, relative frequency, and model segment. (See sample printout in example 5.)
8. *ASSIGN* each parent model (source tag) to one or more groups. *TAG* each model segment with group tag.
9. *LIST* on tape for further processing, each model segment with group tag, source tag, frequency and relative frequency; listing once for each group assignment.

55

10. *SORT* on group tag, then model segment.

11. *CALCULATE* relative frequency of each model segment within its group.

12. *PRINT* for each group, each model segment with mean relative frequency in the group and relative frequency in each parent model (source).

CATALOGUE NUMBER 62

FREQUENCY	PERCENT	PATTERN
1	0.43	-12
4	1.73	-7
3	1.30	-5
6	2.60	-4
19	8.23	-3
54	23.38	-2
20	8.66	-1
15	6.49	0
36	15.58	1
10	4.33	2
6	2.60	3
8	3.46	4
8	3.46	5
1	0.43	7
2	0.87	8
		12

FREQUENCY	PERCENT	PATTERN
3	1.30	
6	2.60	
1	0.43	
3	1.30	
4	1.73	
3	1.30	
2	0.87	
1	0.43	
8	3.46	
7	3.03	
4	1.73	
6	2.60	
5	2.16	
4	1.73	
4	1.73	
1	0.43	
1	0.43	
2	0.87	
12	5.19	
2	0.87	
3	1.30	
1	0.43	
5	2.16	
3	1.30	

Example 5

56

The procedure outlined above can be generalized. The model segment extracted in step 1 may be of any type and may be transformed to any level of classification. Several kinds of segments may be extracted, given a class tag and processed together. The source tag in step 3 may refer to any population from which the model segment is extracted, be it a single composition as in the example or a group of compositions from a single style community or a section of a composition. The output in step 12 may be used to discover stylistic trends by allowing each column to represent a larger style community than a single composition. The comparisons between the style communities represented by the columns may be based upon chronological, geographical or musical criteria or any combination of specifications which delimit the source population.

In the following section a program which yields the distribution of items within a class will be presented. This program yields the distribution of spacing of each chord class used in a composition. The principal steps in this process are as follows:

1. *EXTRACT* all model segments meeting segment specifications from selected compositions stored on MUMODL LIBRARY TAPE. (Segment Specifications: all pitches occurring simultaneously at each note inception.)

2. *TRANSFORM* each segment into the standard form (transposed, T = the negative value of the lowest pitch).

3. *TAG* each segment with classification tag. Classification tag is the segment, transformed into a pitch class set in normal order.

4. *LIST* on tape for further processing, each model segment in standard form with class tag.

5. *COUNT* frequency of each segment and each tag.

6. *CALCULATE* frequency distribution of the model segments in standard form within each classification.

57

7. *PRINT* each pitch class set in normal order with frequency distribution of chord which shows spacing. (See sample printout in example 6.)

PC SET	FREQ	SETTING				FREQ DIST PER CEN
0 3 7	173	0	0	3	7	03
		0	3	7	12	05
		0	3	12	19	08
		0	4	9	9	05
		0	4	9	16	07
		0	5	8	12	01
		0	5	12	20	02
		0	7	12	15	12
		0	7	15	24	14
		0	8	12	17	03
		0	9	16	16	03
		0	9	16	21	06
		0	12	15	19	10
		0	12	17	20	02
		0	12	19	27	09
		0	12	20	29	03
		0	16	21	21	07
0 4 7	154	0	0	4	7	01
		0	3	8	8	02
		0	3	8	15	06
		0	3	15	20	09
		0	4	7	12	04
		0	4	12	19	09
		0	5	9	12	01
		0	5	12	21	01
		0	7	12	16	13
		0	7	16	24	16
		0	8	15	15	04
		0	9	12	17	03
		0	12	16	19	11
		0	12	17	21	02
		0	12	19	28	10
		0	15	21	21	08

Example 6

In the following section there will be a discussion of a study which is concerned with the interdependency of two aspects of musical structure. The purpose of this study is to determine if in a collection of melodies there is a dependency between the change of melodic direction and the relative duration of the notes which precede and follow the change of direction. The coincidence of these aspects occur in a segment of three adjacent notes. The pitches of the three notes are classified to indicate if the middle note is a high turning point (HTP), a low turning point (LTP), or not a turning point (NTP), and the durations are classified to indicate if the first and last notes are shorter than, equal to, or longer than the middle note (see example 7, DURATION CLASS SYMBOLS). A two dimensional table is used to tally the frequency of coincidence of the contour and duration class in the model segments (See example 7, TABLE OF CONTOUR AND DURATION CLASS COINCIDENCE).

DURATION CLASS SYMBOLS

LL $(D_1 < D_2$ & $D_3 < D_2)$
EL $(D_1 = D_2$ & $D_3 < D_2)$
GL $(D_1 > D_2$ & $D_3 < D_2)$
LE $(D_1 < D_2$ & $D_3 = D_2)$
EE $(D_1 = D_2$ & $D_3 = D_2)$
GE $(D_1 > D_2$ & $D_3 = D_2)$
LG $(D_1 < D_2$ & $D_3 > D_2)$
EG $(D_1 = D_2$ & $D_3 > D_2)$
GG $(D_1 > D_2$ & $D_3 > D_2)$

D=duration
subscript=ordinal location

TABLE OF CONTOUR AND DURATION CLASS COINCIDENCE

	NTP	HTP	LTP
LL			
EL			
GL			
LE			
EE			
GE			
LG			
EG			
GG			

Example 7

The principal steps in this process are as follows:

1. *EXTRACT* the pitch values and duration values for each segment of three adjacent notes from a collection of melody models.

59

2. Process each model segment as follows:
   a. *CLASSIFY* pitches according to contour table.
   b. I = the contour tabular location.
   c. *CLASSIFY* durations according to duration table.
   d. J = the duration tabular location.
   e. *ADD* 1 to CELL (I, J) in the CLASS COINCIDENCE TABLE.

3. In an array which corresponds to the class coincidence table *CALCULATE* the expected frequencies under the nule hypothesis that the contour class of a model segment is independent of its duration class.

4. *CALCULATE* the coefficient of contingency for each row and for the entire table.

This process can be generalized. Any classification may be substituted for the contour and duration classes and the number of items in each class may be variable. The number of classes can also be increased and more sophisticated statistical analysis employed.

In the procedures described so far there has been no visual examination of the music once the problem has been defined. At certain stages of a study it may be necessary or useful to examine printed scores. In the following section a procedure will be described which produces data to aid in the visual study of scores. The purpose of this program is to produce an index of model segments of a particular kind which occur in a population of compositions. The principal steps in this process are as follows:

1. *EXTRACT* all model segments meeting segment specifications.

2. *TRANSFORM* each segment into a standard form.

3. *TAG* each segment with source tags referencing parent composition, measure, and voice.

60

4. *LIST* for further processing each segment with its source tags.

5. *SORT* first on model segments then on source tags.

6. *PRINT* each model segment followed by list of sources.

One approach to the study of musical style involves large collections of musical examples which are treated statistically. Computers are eminently suited for such operations. The procedures described in this paper were presented as concrete indicators of the potential utility of automated information processing for such studies. Utilizing the information processing power of computers, style communities of any size may be described more thoroughly and with more accuracy than has heretofore been possible and by comparison of groups of compositions stylistic evolution of great intricacy can be described with a good level of reliability. The study of musical style may then be on the threshold of a new era, one in which the objectives are perhaps more grandiose and yet more detailed than has been previously feasible. However much must be done to realize this potential. It seems to me that a period of development may still be required before a significant corpus of computer-implemented stylistic studies is produced, a period in which generalized music models are stockpiled, in which generalized programs are developed, in which a theoretical basis for this kind of work is formulated and refined, and in which some prototype studies are completed. The length of this development period may depend upon the intensity of the effort and the support it receives. It need not be long and it remains to be seen where it will lead.

Programming a Computer for Music Composition

by
Lejaren A. Hiller

A practical way of writing music with a computer—or without a computer, for that matter—is to throw away undesirable choices made in a stochastic process. What is a stochastic process? It is basically an operation in which elements are chosen sequentially according to some probability distribution. In other words, when we employ a stochastic process, we do work in a probabilistic world. I think this concept is important not only from the standpoint that it leads us to the writing of useful computer programs for composing music, but also because it raises an important philosophical point. Specifically, it leads us away from the idea that a musical structure must always be some sort of deterministically conceived entity. I am sure you have all heard the expression of the idea that one must always be concerned with the inevitability of a given chord resolution, of a given sequence, of a given unfolding of a musical structure, and so on. In contrast to this rather restrictive type of musical thinking, I propose that we can also define other classes of musical communication systems in which a particular composition is but one example from a large class of essentially similar compositions. If certain elements are changed within the matrix of elements making up a system of this sort, a different composition in terms of fine detail may be produced, but its gross properties taken as a whole remain essentially the same, and its effect upon the listener also remains essentially the same. In a way, we have here a crude analogy to the kinetic theory of gases, if one wishes for a moment to think about physics. According to this theory, we can predict rather accurately the macroscopic properties of a body of gas, but we cannot determine the particular positions or energy contents of individual molecules within the total body of this same gas.

65

This mention of the kinetic theory of gases brings me to the concept of information as embodied in the mathematical theory of communication. I assume that most of you are familiar by now with the basic idea of this theory that information is defined as a quantitative measure such that high information content is associated with a relatively high degree of disorder, unpredictability or even randomness, and that order is measured by the opposing conjugate property of redundancy. Let me immediately emphasize, however, that when we say a system has high information, high entropy, high disorder, and lack of predictability, we are simply making a statement concerning *how much* information is present, and we are not committing ourselves in any way as to whether this information is to be considered "good" or "bad" in the normal sense. Information theory, as currently formulated, has nothing to do with semantic meaning, i.e., does a message make sense, nor even less does it have anything to do with value, i.e., does a message seem to be significant, important or beautiful. I think it is essential to stress this point at this time because I am occasionally asked, "How can you get a computer to write a piece of good music?" I reply that if I can be told what "good music" is in terms of precise and quantitative algebraic statements, I can produce "good music".

Actually, however, what do we really do to write music with a computer? We first generate random numbers in the computer and associate each random integer with some particular element of a musical structure. These elements are the usual ones of pitches, rhythms, dynamics, playing instructions such as *arco* and *pizzicato*, permissible chord structures, and so on. Second, we subject the chosen random numbers to many tests that are rather like sieves through which the random numbers must be strained. These tests might reflect the constraints of the usual compositional rules, *a priori* rules which merely strike one's fancy, the results of statistical analyses that provide frequency distributions to which one can refer, or even self-generating rules

66

produced in the computer in such a way that a structure is generated and then investigated in order to draw inferences from it to cause the structure to be extended by means of new rules in some sort of logical manner. Third, we assemble our results into units of music or portions thereof. Thus, we are really applying some of the ideas of information theory in an operational and practical way. In effect, what we do is to generate a communication system of high information content—the random music generating process—and then reduce the information content of this system to what ever degree we desire or can formulate.

Let me now consider some of the specific ideas we use when we think about music composition in terms of programming. I refer specifically to our first experiments in writing an assembly language for music composition which we call MUSICOMP. We are still working on this language, and it is by no means complete. Moreover, its users still must know a specific computer language, namely SCATRE, to use it at all. However, we are gradually eliminating such defects and difficulties in MUSI-COMP as we slowly build it up to have its own terminology. MUSICOMP will eventually contain a large number of mnemonic symbols derived from conventional music. As one simple example of this kind of terminology, we already have a stock of ordinary punched cards printed with the titles "Xylophone", "Trumpet in B flat", etc. Each of these cards gives all the constraints for its instrument in terms of playing range, playing styles, dynamics range, and so on. These can be automatically consulted whenever MUSICOMP is used.

The basic idea of MUSICOMP is the following: As a working hypothesis, we say that the procedural logic for composition can be distinguished, at least to a first approximation, from all the specific decisions we must make in reference to establishing any particular musical style we might desire to work with. In other words, we propose that when one thinks musically, one uses a process which can be abstracted as pure musical logic as such.

This hypothesis applies whether we write twelve-tone music, random music, 16th-century counterpoint, 19th-century tonal music or whatever. If this hypothesis is valid, we can build a general compiler for music composition and utilize this compiler to write programs which will assemble music compositions which can range from highly unpredictable to completely deterministic in content. Once again, let me emphasize that the style choice is up to the programmer. In effect, we must make a long series of decisions which must be set up in an appropriate operational sequence. Then, each decision process in turn must be used to consult a series of reference statements which tell precisely how the decision is to be made. For example, let us assume that we are writing a conventional piece of music, a melody with an accompanying harmonic structure. To do this, we might set up a series of questions which go from the most general to the most specific in terms of decision making. In effect, we break down the decision process into a number of sub-decisions. First we might ask: "At what structural level is this decision going to be made?" In other words, is it something that affects a large section of music or only one note? Second, we might ask: "What is the harmonic structure for this particular level?" Third, we might ask: "Where does it belong in the measure, and how long is it going to last?" Finally, we might ask: "What is the actual harmony?" To answer all these questions, we have the program consult information stored in the computer memory. The same sort of thing is then done to produce the melody and any other components of the musical structure that need to be composed.

MUSICOMP currently incorporates several basic categories of materials: (1) A main routine that is normally written in either MUSICOMP mnemonics or in SCATRE by the composer. A main routine may be rather short since it may be only concerned with major decisions. On the other hand, it may be quite extensive if the compositional desires of the programmer are complex and sophisticated. (2) A growing number of subroutines con-

Simple Example of a Flow Diagram in MUSICOMP

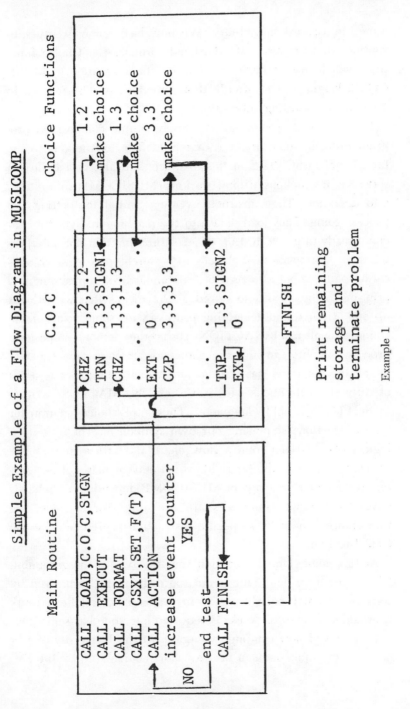

Main Routine	C.O.C	Choice Functions
CALL LOAD,C.O.C,SIGN	CHZ 1,2,1.2	1.2 make choice
CALL EXECUT	TRN 3,3,SIGN1	1.3 make choice
CALL FORMAT	CHZ 1,3,1.3	3.3 make choice
CALL CSX1,SET,F(T)	EXT 0	
CALL ACTION	CZP 3,3,3,3	
increase event counter		
YES	TNP 1,3,SIGN2	
NO end test	EXT 0	
CALL FINISH	FINISH	

Print remaining
storage and
terminate problem

Example 1

69

tained in a subroutine library. We now have some twenty subroutines that are all in standardized formats. (3) Choice functions which are normally written by the composer in MUSICOMP language. (4) Modification functions which are used to alter already existing subroutines.

In Example 1, I show an extremely simple composition program utilizing some of these materials. The instructions to the far left are in SCATRE in this instance, and are, in actuality, a series of instructions calling various MUSICOMP subroutines into operation. These instructions are essential for getting the process going. They load data into the machine and get the machine ready to go. FORMAT is our subroutine that not only provides for storing musical choices in a stereotyped memory allocation pattern, but also provides a standardized alphanumerical print-out of the results so stored. CSX1 means that we will set up one of our sound generating processes for some or all of the compositional results. ACTION starts the actual composition process. We first go into the choice order code (the C.O.C.) which the composer has written and which consists of a series of different instructions which are actually "MACROS" written in SCATRE assembly language. These are choice or transfer type instructions employing our own symbolism. They set up a logical plan derived from a flow chart and utilize in turn the choice functions to the far right which may or may not be written in computer language or MUSICOMP depending on what is desired and what subroutines are available. For example, the first choice is actually a specific instruction represented by the CHZ function.

At this point, I might mention that the type of programming I have just been describing is not too difficult to learn, even by someone not particularly versed in mathematical skills. I think from about four to six weeks is required once one has some general notions of how computers operate. At the University of Illinois, for example, one can take a "short course" run by the De-

70

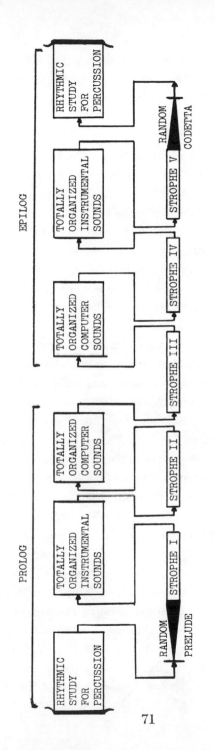

COMPUTER CANTATA

STRUCTURAL PLAN

Example 2

71

partment of Computer Science in which topics such as FOR-TRAN and SCATRE programming are discussed. Once this basic introduction is obtained, one is able to use MUSICOMP in about a month or so.

Now let me turn to some results. In Example 2, I show a diagram of the first piece done with MUSICOMP, namely a piece called *Computer Cantata*. Robert Baker and I wrote an article for *Perspectives of New Music* a couple of years ago in which we discussed this composition in some detail.[1] In the *Computer Cantata*, we ran a number of experiments in which we tried out some ideas primarily to get some of the processes embodied in MUSICOMP going. Although we do not claim that this is a highly sophisticated piece of music in terms of structural flow, nevertheless, we did solve a few basic problems required of almost all compositional projects. For example, we set up a reasonably complex and adaptable rhythm generating program which was used to generate the music that opens and closes the cantata. Second, we produced a couple of examples of totally organized serial music in which all parameters are related to a single twelve-tone row. We followed the procedures used by Boulez to write his *Structures for Two Pianos—Part I* for these two sections of the *Computer Cantata*. Third, we also exploited one type of computer sound generation. This is a real time sound generating process that will be mentioned later on. We wrote two pieces for this in which the harmonic and linear, i.e., the vertical and horizontal-structure depended upon certain probability distributions. Also, we employed a mixture of nine to fifteen notes per octave in equal temperament. In other words, we were interested in exploring scale systems other than twelve tones to the octave. These six units of music comprise the various *Prologs* and *Epilogs* of the *Computer Cantata*.

Finally, the five main structures are the five *Strophes*. Three colleagues on our faculty at Illinois had already analyzed phonemic text—that is to say, spoken text—in terms of the phonemic

72

alphabet.[2] They did this in what is called zeroth to fourth-order analysis. Zeroth-order analysis assumes a simple random model. First-order analysis consists of frequency counts; for example, if we were considering letters of the alphabet, we would count how many *s*'s, how many *e*'s, how many *x*'s, and so on, occur in the sample of text under scrutiny. Then, in second-order analysis, we ask, given the choice of some letter like *e*, what is the probability of the letter *x* following it, or the letter *q*, or the letter *i*, and so on? In third-order analysis, supposing we already have a pair of letters like *ab*, we ask what is the chance of getting a letter such as *f*, or *x*, or *s*, and so forth? Finally, in fourth-order analysis, we seek to determine the probability of the letters following triplets of letters such as *abc*. Thus, we build up models for analysis based upon the assumption of the existence of monograms, digrams, trigrams, and tetragrams. Now, having these frequency distributions, we can synthesize in reverse order. In other words, we can write text or compose music according to probability matrices. And that is precisely what we did to obtain *Strophes I* to *V*, namely, we generated zeroth-order to fourth-order stochastic music set to texts provided by Hultzén, Allen and Miron. *Strophe I*, being zeroth-order, provides a purely random phonemic and musical environment. In *Strophe II*, for the music, we employed frequency counts of rhythms and pitches taken from a sample of Ives' *Three Places in New England*. Continuing, *Strophe III* then consists of digram structures, *Strophe IV* of trigram structures and *Strophe V* of tetragram structures. We thus obtained a progression from high information content to lower information content, following in principle the five synthesized texts provided us. We picked phonemic text to set to music because it is always singable.

Example 3 shows a simple way of picturing probability distributions derived from a conditional probability matrix. Let us assume that we have two probability distributions as shown at the top of the example. The one to the left is the probability of

COMPUTER CANTATA:
MATRIX SYSTEM FOR STOCHASTIC
CONDITIONAL PROBABILITIES

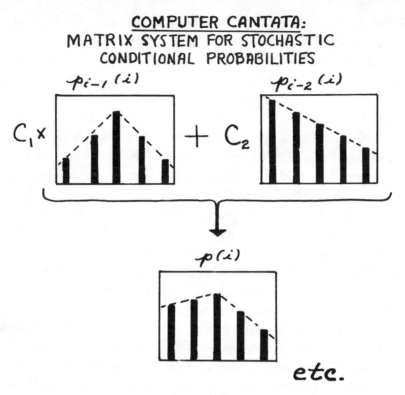

Example 3

choice i, given a previous choice i-1. For example, we might say that i-1 represents a symbol in the middle of a symmetrical distribution of pitches. In this instance, it is most likely that a repeat will occur with the note on each side of the repeat being somewhat less frequent and the notes farther and farther from the repeat being progressively less frequent in occurrence. The distribution to the right is the probability of the choice i in terms of how it depends on the penultimate choice i-2. This distribution has a different shape from the first. When these are multiplied by appropriate constants, C1 and C2, and added together, we obtain the actual probability we will use. It is shown by itself below. It represents an algebraic combination of the other two graphs.

74

COMPUTER CANTATA:

STRUCTURE OF THE INTRODUCTION TO STROPHE I

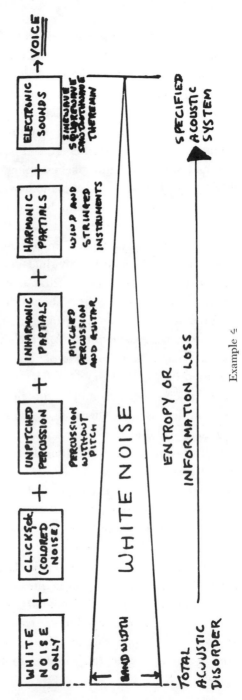

Example 4

Example 4 shows the beginning of *Strophe I*. When planning *Strophe I*, we thought that it might also be interesting to start it with the highest possible acoustic information content, rather than with our defined scalar system. Consequently, we added a little prelude to *Strophe I* which starts with white noise. White noise acoustically has maximum information content because it contains all possible sounds. It consists of all audible frequencies and sounds roughly like escaping steam. Parenthetically, I might note that here we have another interesting question about probability distributions, namely, the question of the degree of subdivision of our musical materials. White noise is sound subdivided randomly on such a microstructural level that the ear cannot ordinarily detect individual events occurring inside this noise pattern. To what degree then does one subdivide a musical structure and to what degree should this structure be random or determinate? This is an important point to think about when we work with stochastic music, or for that matter, any kind of chance composition. For example, let us consider a composition like John Cage's *Williams Mix*. The recorded segments of sound Cage spliced together into eight channels of tape are rather short on the average. Therefore, when all these sounds are mixed together, we obtain a rather dense and uniform texture. Although this music might be considered to be tending toward the white noise extreme of the acoustic spectrum, i.e., toward high information, it still sounds quite different from white noise itself, not because it might be less random than white noise in terms of how its ingredients are mixed, but rather because its materials are not chopped up as fine as white noise. In contrast to this, we can, of course, also take large sections of music and assemble them into random sequences. The results would not seem at all the same as *Williams Mix* simply because of the fact that we did indeed utilize larger structures and mix them. Cage, of course, has done this in other compositions, as have many other composers recently. Another quite different, but obvious

76

case in point, would be Mozart's *Musikalishes Würfelspiel,* in which whole measures are selected by throwing dice, which incidentally, is a first-order stochastic process since the results are *not* equiprobable, but are independent of previous throws. This composition sounds much more organized, not only because the sequence must fit a previously defined outline, but also because the subdivision of the materials is rather coarse.

However, I must return to the *Computer Cantata.* As I already mentioned, we started *Strophe I* with white noise. We then differentiated this total spectrum bit by bit into discrete acoustic events producing first colored noise, that is to say, ordinary noises with discrete frequency-bands and transients. Next, we scored in unpitched percussion, which is still very much noise. Then, a couple of measures later, we permitted sounds with inharmonic partials, then sounds with harmonic partials, then electronic sounds with precisely defined overtone structures, and finally the entry of the voice. At this point, we enter *Strophe I* proper. I consider this to be an amusing little demonstration of how one becomes able to distinguish specific events arising out of a matrix in which individual events are too tiny to be perceived. Note, incidentally, that the voice part in all the strophes is quite difficult to sing, since it is a single line set up against a complex pattern of independently generated sounds. Also, instead of just duple and triple rhythms, we employ subdivisions of the rhythm up to septuplets. Actually, we could have added groups of nine, eleven and thirteen, or higher had we so desired, but we felt this was sufficient at the time.

Let me now skip ahead and consider the fourth-order music embodied in *Strophe V.* Here, we begin to get some sense of phrasing. In other words, if the vocalist is singing a note, the tendency is for her to continue singing until she finally comes to a pause and then she is likely to rest for a while. We also get some sense of some intervals being preferred to others. However, there is still no correlation between the various melodic lines

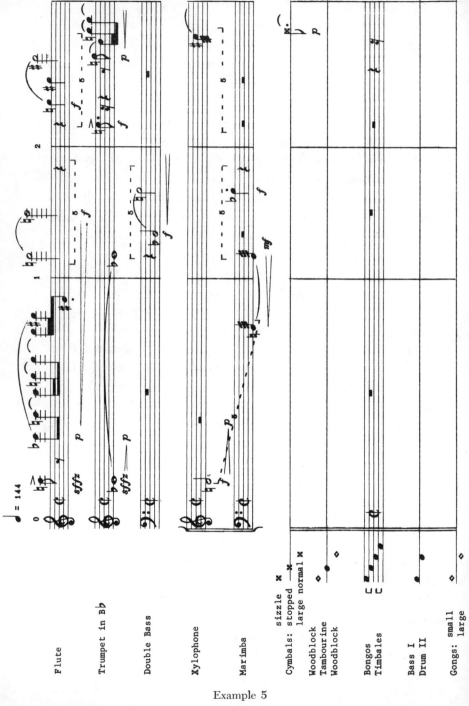

Example 5

even in *Strophe V.* In other words, whatever the flute plays has no relationship in any *direct* way to what the voice does; it does relate only indirectly in terms of the probability distribution. In the *Computer Cantata,* we thus have in *Strophes I* to V what might be labelled heterophony. Vertical relationships are something we are working on in the new piece, *Algorithms I* that I will turn to briefly in a moment.

The *Strophes* also obviously do not change in terms of their musical content from beginning to end, but only from one to the next, because there is no change of information level set in any of them. We wished to conform to the text we were setting, which was fixed in this same manner. I must assure you that this is by no means necessary. Other sections of this piece have structurally variable information levels within given movements. This is particularly true, once again, of the new piece I just referred to that we are now composing.

In Example 5, I show the opening of *Sonoriferous Loops* which was written in 1964 by Herbert Brün. I thought you would like to see a bit of the actual score of a piece written with a computer. This composition is also one that was composed by means of stochastic note generating processes.

In Example 6, I show one kind of structural logic we are currently developing. While composing, I do not believe that a composer simply proceeds from one musical event to the next in a literal time sequence. It seems to me that he jumps ahead, backs and fills, then perhaps jumps ahead a little bit again, and constantly moves all around in relation to the structural plan of the music being composed. When I myself think in musical terms as I compose any kind of music, I often seem to think first in terms of the large structure. For example, a certain melodic idea might occur to me, and I block it in and then I work back, perhaps filling in some structure that precedes it. Perhaps on another occasion, I might work out one section of music precisely and then jump ahead. I very likely might do this in work-

79

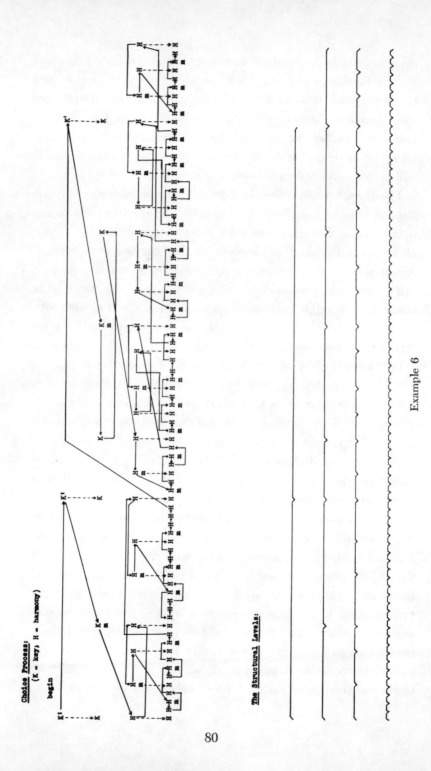

Example 6

ing with a sonata form, for example. I might write out an exposition and then go ahead and do the recapitulation before I fill in all the intervening development. In other words, I suggest that a composer moves back and forth in the time dimension; consequently, we must have a decision plan worked out to operate in a similar way in a computer.

Let me now make a few brief remarks regarding the new composition referred to above. It is called *Algorithms I*. I am writing substantial parts of this in collaboration with Antonio Leal, a graduate student in mathematics currently working with me at Illinois. The plan of this work involves three movements of two, three and four minutes duration respectively. They are entitled "The Decay of Information", "Icosahedron" and "Incorporations". The first movement is a study of the control of information content level within a movement by means of varying probability distributions. The second movement is a study of how to compose a complete twelve-tone piece by means of one single program. The third movement is a study of how to impose a substantial number of standard compositional techniques upon a stochastically generated musical matrix. Let me restrict my remarks here, however, to the first movement only, because it is the one movement so far completed in its entirety (as of April, 1966).

One important feature of this piece is that we found it useful to insert a "governor program" to the left of the programming structure of the type shown in Example 1. This governor program controls the main routine and changes it so that it provides the nearest approximation we have thus far to something which permits us to produce in the computer an extended composition which changes as it develops. In other words, it provides some sense of starting somewhere and going somewhere else. It changes the instructions in the main routine because it is returned to as often as required to do this. In the present instance, it does not yet provide the back and fill plan outlined above, but this is where such logic will be provided.

81

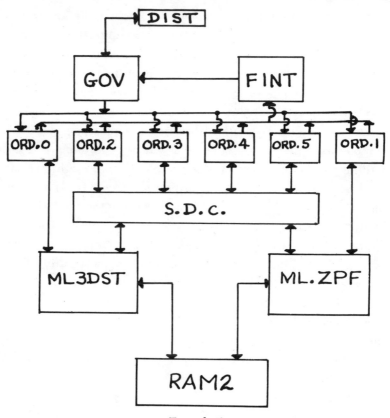

Example 7

In Example 7, I show a flow chart which reveals how this governor program is used to control the structure of the first movement of *Algorithms I*. In this instance, the governor is used to control the degree to which, in each of the twelve instrumental lines in this composition, zeroth-order to fourth-order stochastic control is developed for the choice of parameters. We have provided a number of boxes in the flow chart which are a particular kind of stochastic order boxes. In the present instance, these are limited to 0, 1, 2, 3, and 4, but actually could go as high as we might want. In reality, of course, these are self-contained subroutines which we have labelled ORD.0, ORD.1, ORD.2, ORD.3, and ORD.4. As these subroutines are activated, they in turn are used to set up tests by means of the network of connecting links to the boxes shown in the bottom of the diagram.

The tests determine whether the results conform to what the governor dictates. Both into the governor and out of it are also provided logical connections to a consulting memory for what I should like to call a macro-control of the whole movement. In this particular piece, we decided to have the governor consult for information content level at any particular instance in time in the piece, i.e., for the amount of order we want. It consults by means of a subroutine that employs Shannon's equation in order to compute information content continually as a control over the whole process. Finally, for the sake of simplicity in this first movement, we utilized a scheme in which we plotted information versus time by means of a simple exponential function which decays with respect to time. We caused the information content to drop from 100%, i.e., maximum information for the system, down to 50%, a reasonable value, at the termination of the movement. We obtained this by simply having the twelve instruments have different levels of stochastic control of pitch choices at each instant in time. The number of instruments which have zeroth-order, first-order, second-order, third-order or fourth-order control at any point was determined in turn by the information level at that particular instant in time. Then, the distribution of all the instruments in terms of the order-number was set by a distribution function that kept changing with respect to time. Consequently, we had a gradual evolution of the music from a disordered to a somewhat organized pattern. Of course, one can have any shape one wishes for an information plot of this sort. For example, it can move up and down so it can reach points where it seems to be more ambiguous and possess higher information and become chaotic and then resolve and come back to a level of greater order. This is something we propose to do in later movements of the composition.

I should now like to take up a final point. I want to discuss briefly sound synthesis with computers, since this has been omitted so far in any of the presentations given at this meeting. There are two basic methods for generating sound with a computer. One very simple process depends on the fact that the computer has an accumulator register which is divided into bits. Since a computer adds and subtracts numbers at a given rate depending on its clock, we can cause the lefthand bit of the accumulator register, which represents symbolically plus and minus, to change from one to zero at any desired rate depending on the size of a number being repeatedly added over and over again to itself. Taking a simple case, suppose we have only three-bit numbers. As we go from 0 to 7 decimally, we go from 000 to 111 in terms of the binary numbers that are used in a computer. If we then add yet another 1, the accumulator overflows, the 1 shifts left out of the accumulator and is lost. Meanwhile, the high order bit reverts back to zero. Consequently, we have a square wave generated by the high-order bit. This is an actual pulse which can be taken off the accumulator and amplified. Moreover, this sound can be filtered, if we wish, and otherwise modified. Even though this sound source is not very good because the available timbre choices are rather limited, the sounds so produced can be generated in real time, which is a distinct advantage to a composer who might wish to modify sounds as he hears them being produced. The details of this process have been described in an article by J. L. Divilbiss.[3]

A much more sophisticated and better way of generating sound is by digital-to-analog conversion, a process first worked out by J. R. Pierce, Max Mathews, and their colleagues at Bell Telephone Laboratories. Actually, we can not only synthesize sounds by digital-to-analog conversion, but conversely, we can also analyze real sounds by analog-to-digital conversion, the reverse process. Let us examine how such processes work. Any sound, complex or simple, can be represented by a plot of amplitude versus time. This is what is represented by the groove in a phonograph record, for example. Similarly, the physical substance inside an ordinary audio amplifier is an electrical analog to sound; it is not the sound itself, it is only an analog voltage. This fluctuating analog voltage can be sampled, divided up, and converted into numbers. With a fine sampling rate, we can get a very close step approximation to this signal in terms of long lists of numbers. The band-width theorem states that if the sampling rate is twice the band-width of the sample being analyzed, we will have an essentially noise-free system in terms of quantization noise. For practical audio purposes, let us take 20,000 cycles per second as the upper limit of hearing for the normal ear, an upper limit also above the response of even high quality tape recorders. So, if we employ 40,000 samples per second, we will have a system which is free of quantizing noise arising from the sampling rate. With a computer, we can easily generate 40,000 numbers a second which will be proportional to a voltage that fluctuates with respect to time. If these numbers in the computer, which are normally stored on digital tape, are then run through a digital-to-analog converter, we obtain a step approximation of a wave form which is good enough so that the ear cannot detect the difference between this and the real thing. There are certain restrictions, however. One restriction is that we also have to sub-divide the amplitude scale. The sub-division which seems to be necessary is about 12 to 13 bits. Twelve seems to be marginal, but 13 apparently works very nicely as far as we can tell at present. A second problem involves what is called "fold-over". This simply means that if we compute a wave form in the computer like a sawtooth wave which has a complete spectrum of overtones, the higher harmonics of this wave beat against the sampling frequency of 40,000 cps. This in turn generates a large number of sum and difference tones which fold back in between the harmonics of the generated sound, producing very disturbing inharmonic partials which can actually be louder than the original sound.

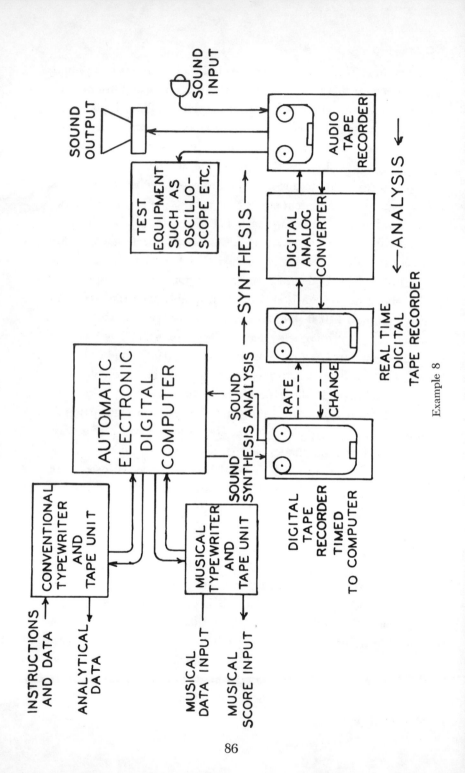

SOUND INPUT

SOUND OUTPUT

TEST EQUIPMENT SUCH AS OSCILLO-SCOPE ETC.

AUDIO TAPE RECORDER

DIGITAL ANALOG CONVERTER

← ANALYSIS ←

SYNTHESIS →

REAL TIME DIGITAL TAPE RECORDER

RATE ─ ─ CHANGE

AUTOMATIC ELECTRONIC DIGITAL COMPUTER

SOUND SYNTHESIS ANALYSIS

SOUND SYNTHESIS ANALYSIS

DIGITAL TAPE RECORDER TIMED TO COMPUTER

CONVENTIONAL TYPEWRITER AND TAPE UNIT

MUSICAL TYPEWRITER AND TAPE UNIT

INSTRUCTIONS AND DATA

ANALYTICAL DATA

MUSICAL DATA INPUT

MUSICAL SCORE INPUT

Example 8

86

As I said, one can also analyze sounds by the reverse process of analog-to-digital conversion. A number of people are now engaged in such research including the people at Bell Telephone Laboratories, James Tenney at Yale, and ourselves at the University of Illinois. For example, David Freedman at Illinois recently took samples of tones produced by five real instruments, namely, a clarinet, saxophone, bassoon, trumpet, and violin, ran them through an analog-to-digital converter into our ILLIAC II and analyzed them by Fourier analysis not only for steady state properties, but also for transient characteristics. He was particularly interested in establishing precise specifications for the parameters to enter into a generalized Fourier equation for the attack portions of the time envelopes of the sounds produced by these instruments. He did this for up to twenty partials of these harmonic tones. He found out that at least a couple of these instruments such as the trumpet and the saxophone, also have inharmonicities in the attack portions of their time envelopes. If he omitted these upon resynthesis from his data, the synthesized product did not sound as much like a trumpet or saxophone as when these inharmonic partials were present.

To summarize, in Example 8, I show what I think hypothetical compositional and analytical computing machines ought to be like. At the input stage, musical data input and output in music notation and instructions and analytical data in ordinary notation are entered into and retrieved from the computer. I might point out that this illustration was prepared when we thought a music typewriter was the best way of doing this. As I think everyone realizes now, photographic and scanning methods are much better than typewriters; consequently, we too plan to change hardware, but we have not, of course, changed our plan conceptually. Sound synthesis and analysis is also a reversible process as I have just described. Sound is first stored in digital form on digital tape. We convert the sound through a digital-to-

87

analog converter and then store the result on an audio tape. Conversely, we can take audio sounds and run them back into the system via analog-to-digital conversion as shown.

REFERENCES

1. L. A. Hiller, Jr., and R. A. Baker, *"Computer Cantata:* An Investigation of Compositional Procedure", *Perspectives of New Music,* 3: 62, 1964.

2. L. S. Hultzén, J. Allen, Jr., and M. S. Miron, *Tables of Transitional Frequencies of English Phonemes,* University of Illinois Press, Urbana, Illinois, 1964.

3. J. L. Divilbiss, "Real-time Generation of Music with a Digital Computer", *J. Music Theory,* 8: 99, 1964.

An Introduction to the Information
Processing Capabilities of
the Computer

by
Charles C. Cook

Why am I here if you are musicians and I am an engineer? I cannot tell you where computers and music shall meet and where they shall never meet. However, I hope to outline for you the *information processing* capabilities of computers. From this outline and from the other very interesting papers you have heard earlier today, it is my hope that you can further envision and explore this proposition of "music meets computer".

Any art, any science, any task is partially composed of the need to process information, in fact sometimes heavily burdened, with the need to process information—that is, to read, correct, re-arrange, calculate, print, and save those symbols required to communicate thoughts between two or more persons or between devices to which have been imparted a portion of the knowledge of man or the universe.

We know that the form of the symbol and the syntax used to combine these symbols can highly interact with the efficiency and accuracy of the thought transmitted. We know that two entirely different forms of symbols may suffice equally well to communicate the same thought; e.g., half-note middle C, the letter X, the series of pulses 10110, a voltage level of 0.72 milivolts, two holes in predetermined positions of a punched card may all transmit a portion of a thought with equal, or varying, levels of efficiency.

Whether one be studying music theory or music history, or composing, or instructing others to use a musical instrument, there is much information processing involved. Perhaps a very sizeable portion of this processing is forever beyond the capabilities of computers, but we have seen today that there are definitely portions of this information processing which conform to

91

existing technology well enough to already have been partially automated. So let us take a look into this black box called a computer—or more properly an electronic data processing *system*.

There are five basic functional portions of a digital computer system. The center of the system is the memory where there are numerous symbols stored. This storage may be implemented in various physical forms, principally the magnetic core, a donut shaped ferric oxide core of perhaps .020 inch outer diameter. These cores can be arranged in any one of many fashions so that their combinations of clockwise and counterclockwise magnetism can be made to represent alphabetic characters, numerical characters of any one of several different "arithmetics", or special symbols such as parenthesis, commas, etc. These characters may be further combined to form "words", a string of typically 5-8 alphabetic characters or a string of 8-10 numerical digits. A computer memory will usually store from 4,000 to 32,000 of these words.

The second basic portion of a computer is the input section where symbols are "read" by a physical or electronic device such as a punched card reader and transmitted at speeds such as 20,000 to 120,000 characters per second to the computer memory, where they are properly converted to a series of "bits", that is, magnetism of the cores in clockwise or counterclockwise positions.

Similarly there is an output portion of the computer where the reverse process is performed with printed paper being the final form often implemented.

A big system may have numerous different input and output devices. Certain of these devices, such as magnetic tape drives, may store information in forms entirely unreadable to the human and hence in reality serve as an extension of the computer memory and are often entitled "storage devices".

A fourth portion of the computer is composed of the logic and arithmetic accumulators, adders, registers, etc. It is in this portion where information may be added, multiplied, compared with other information, tested for sign, or perhaps re-arranged. Processing in these devices occurs at rates up to more than a million times per second.

The fifth and most vital portion is the control section where the circuitry is located which instructs the card reader to read, the printer to print, the adder to add, etc. The instructions to this section are referred to as the program and are stored in the memory along with the information in a manner such that it is very easy to treat instructions as data or to treat data as instructions. Although this *"stored-program concept"* at first appears as a very easy way to "garbage-up" the processing (i.e., miscalculate or mistreat data and/or instructions), it is the backbone of the digital computer's power and it creates, philosophically speaking, the difference between a calculator and a computer. Although this concept did not appear in digital data processing devices until after World War II, it is now very standard.

It is very important to note that computers spend very little time "computing". Most of the time in most applications is spent in reading, storing, re-arranging, re-formating, and writing data. This is true even in a large portion of the so-called "scientific" applications.

I have failed to cite one capability of a computer which is rapidly coming to the forefront. That is, it can control other devices such as lathes, assembly lines, steel mills, or sound-generators. It is this capability to which some of you look with great expectation.

I have also failed to cite what a computer does *not* do. Except within the limitations aforementioned, it cannot *think*. That is, it does not possess the ability to peruse a set of information and create a set of instructions or a set of answers which contain any more intellect than is contained in its programming, which was devised by man. I have now the need to define the word "intellect" without using a form of the verb "think". I shall leave this

93

potential vicious circle to the philosophers and continue the subject of computer usage, as my engineering background prompts.

A moment of digression is necessary to point out that I have been discussing "digital" computers. Of lesser general interest, but of great importance to problem solvers and control computer implementers who deal with varying rate processes is the subject of analog computers. We have seen the information storage and processing capabilities of a *digital* computer are always discrete in nature. Philosophically the digital computer could be replaced by a large number of on/off type switches. Conversely, the analog computer is a combination of devices, typically electronic, which represent information as a point on a scale possessing an infinity of points; e.g., the voltage of a circuit may represent gallons per minute of a chemical flow and this voltage may vary anywhere between say -1 and 9 volts. Generally speaking, analog computers are applied primarily by mathematicians and physical scientists to a much smaller class of information processing (and control) applications than are digital computers.

Coming to the forefront today are combinations of digital and analog computers, called hybrid computers. Although they possess very great power, they are primarily the tool of only the most persevering computist for some years to come.

Although digital computer development began in the late thirties, few existed prior to 1955. Today there are about 33,000 installed by twenty-five U. S. based manufacturers and several thousand more have been produced elsewhere. Another 16,000 are related to be "on order" by these U. S. manufacturers. Digital computers cost from $5,000 to $8,000,000 averaging about 1/3 million dollars. Monthly rental rates are about 1/40 to 1/50 of the selling price. Nearly all can be rented for periods ranging from a few months upward.

Ten years ago the decision of which computer to acquire was much easier than today because of the few number of models available. (There are now perhaps 200 models.) Furthermore, acquisition today is vastly complicated because one must select from hundreds of peripheral devices available. In order to indicate the great capabilities and flexibility one finds, I shall cite a few such devices:

1. Random disk file units which may store or re-read within a half-second or less any information (string of characters) from a file of up to several hundred million characters. These disk files are sometimes removable mechanically so that other files may be inserted into the driving mechanism by the operator within a minute or so.

2. The memory of the computer can communicate with sequential files in the form of magnetic tape at speeds up to nearly a million characters per second. One reel of tape may store typically 10 million characters and as many as 50-100 million characters. Of course, reels are easily mounted and dismounted on these machines, and a storeroom of 2,000 magnetic tape reels is not unusual.

3. Random magnetic card devices containing ferric oxide coated cards of about 6 x 10 inches can store files containing up to billions of characters in size. A half second could elapse while the card is sought, but their transmission rates are very high once they are found: A typical rate may be ¼ million characters per second. Obviously, these files ought to be sequential within categories in order to avoid constant "seeking" of the cards.

4. Magnetic drums are cylinders from 6 to 36 inches in diameter which can store a few million characters on their magnetic surface and can transmit or receive hundreds of thousands of characters per second from the computer memory.

5. If completely random access to data in a large file is required, highest speeds can be achieved by using the more expensive large magnetic core memories of a million or so digits.

6. Punched card readers and punches are very common devices and handle as high as 1,200 and 400 cards per minute respectively.

95

7. Punched paper tape handlers are by far the cheapest devices for storing or reading information, but they have transmission rates only in the hundreds of characters per second.

8. Devices which print on paper range from 10-15 characters per second for typewriters to 1,200 lines per minute for line printers.

Of course, the list is much longer. Equipment has been perfected in so many areas that a manufacturer can match your needs very well. The important point to remember when selecting storage devices is that total size of file, speed of access, and degree of random accessibility sought, all tend to increase the cost. On the other hand, use of a slow device such as a paper tape reader or a faster but strictly sequential device such as a magnetic tape drive may cause the memory and control sections of the computer (often called main frame or central processing unit) to be severely delayed and hence *total* processing cost can easily increase when the lesser expensive devices are attached. A computer systems analyst with a rather heavy technical background is required to properly balance the selection of the system configuration against the needs and finances of an organization desiring to acquire a computer system.

Information processing capabilities are progressing so rapidly today that only the very most farsighted philosopher can begin to predict their influence within the next generation. As an example of a related subject, "information retrieval", I have a 2 x 2 inch micro-slide which contains the complete text of the Holy Bible—1,245 pages. It serves to suggest how drastically we may find some of our age-old institutions such as libraries to be changed.

Let us now take a closer look at the manner in which a person programs the computer; i.e., how one creates these instructions which are stored in the memory of the computer and then individually fed to the control section and "executed". When these instructions are in a form such that they appear as a sequence of numbers, each of which has explicitly defined meaning to the circuitry of the computer, they are said to be in "machine language" or "object code". However, it is a very tedious process to write these codes in the language of the machine and hence this task is nearly always avoided now by most programmers. Furthermore it is also avoided because there is usually no compatibility of these codes from one machine to another, and hence a machine language program is highly susceptible to obsolence.

Since 1957 it has rapidly become the practice to describe the instructions to the computer in languages that more closely resemble algebra or English. Very often these languages are such that one statement may represent many machine language instructions—a feature which entitles the language to be entitled "a higher level language". The most popular algebraic type languages are Fortran and Algol, the former being slightly easier too learn and much more popular at the present time. The latter is a more compact language and is better accepted as a universal language for mathematical procedures.

Cobol is the most popular English-type language, but it has much less acclaim than Fortran at the present time. A typical Cobol statement could read:

IF TOTAL-EARNINGS LESS THAN SOCIAL-SECURITY-MAXIMUM-OF-5400 THEN COMPUTE SOCIAL-SECURITY-DEDUCTION EQUALS EARNINGS TIMES SOCIAL-SECURITY-RATE-4-PERCENT.

The same statement in Fortran might appear as:

IF (TOTERN.LT. SSMAX) SSDED=EARN°SSRATE

Although Cobol statements can be written in a more readable fashion it is very wrong to say that anyone who can read English can program a computer in Cobol. Furthermore, it is improper to state that a Cobol program by itself represents good documentation. Although it is mathematically sufficient, it is usually still quite difficult to follow unless other documentation features accompany the Cobol statements.

Other lower level languages also exist such as SPS, Autocoder, MAP, etc., which are generally labeled "assembly" languages. These languages are more difficult to learn and to implement, but permit a fuller usage of the computer and sometimes improve the speed or space efficiency of the program. Generally speaking, it is highly unlikely that you would need these more machine oriented symbolic assembly languages, and it is probably better to resort to the use of a programming specialist when you need a subroutine written at such a level.

But, I have not answered your likely question, "Which of the 'higher-level' languages is better?" A worldwide universal answer to this question may not be found any sooner than the worldwide universal brand of automobile. The answer is a function of your needs and the environment of your computer center. All things being equal, which they usually aren't, I would recommend Fortran as the starting point. Probably some sixty to one hundred hours of study, supervised if possible, permits one to gain the necessary proficiency to use the computer frequently, but with only moderate efficiency form the computer's point of view. After accomplishing proficiency in one language, the time required to learn a second, a third, etc., programming language becomes quite small.

I am inclined to recommend Fortran because of the likelihood of its availability, the simple nature of its statements, the probability that qualified help is available, the wealth of the textbook material, and the fact that it does not contain many specialized features found in a language such as Cobol, which was designed primarily for commercial applications.

I have failed to clarify a very important point: no computer exists which has circuits that understand Fortran or Cobol. Only

98

when a very elaborate program called a "compiler" is loaded into the computer's memory is it possible for the computer to accept the Fortran or Cobol statements. This elaborate program converts these statements into machine language—a process referred to as "compilation". Then at a later time, perhaps less than a second later, this machine language "object program" is executed.

Considerable confusion exists today as to the value of learning a computer language such as Fortran. That is, many feel that such knowledge is sufficient to solve all of your problems which may be susceptible to computer handling. This is very wrong. The complete process of problem definition and solution when a computer is employed is such that it will be rare in meaningful applications if the portion of the time required to do the coding, i.e., write the Fortran or Cobol statements, ever exceeds 15% of the total time involved. And this percentage decreases as the proficiency of the programmer or the complexity of the problem increases.

What then occupies the rest of your time when you are "programming"? It is first necessary to point out that I am using the term "programming" to encompass all work from earliest decision to implement the computer until final answers are produced. Usually one finds that this work is subdivided into such phases as problem analysis, programming, coding, computer operation, etc. I do not want to expend time here bringing these terms into my presentation, but I do want to cover what I refer to as the "twelve steps of programming". They are:

1. One must carefully set forth the objectives of the problem, i.e., what is to be obtained. This statement must not be subjective nor in any way ambiguous.

2. One must cite the scope and limitations to be implemented. For example, the maximum number of notes per line or minimum number of lines of music score, etc., which will be permitted. Many of these restrictions may appear obvious at first, but later

work may create a need to change them. In any event, failure to cite limitations is one of the largest causes of program malfunction. Few constraints are desirable at first, but often it is necessary to add others later to avoid excessive time or cost.

3. Review what is available in the form of:
   a.) Data which can be processed by the computer and which will be known *before* the program is to be processed.
   b.) Previous programs and subprograms.
   c.) Theory of the subject at hand.

4. Define all symbols to be used. Be mnemonic but not prolific. Failure to carefully define variables and other quantities early in the programming process turns out to be a very large source of trouble later.

5. Flow chart the problem in a manner such that *absolutely* no ambiguity remains as to any step of the problem solution. Although when one is at the novice level the value of flow charts is obscure, progression to a more sophisticated level of computer application demands flow charting. Standard symbol templates are available which greatly enhance your chances of getting help when trouble persists in the program. The flow chart is also an index. It not only is a guide to the routes through the programming, but it proves to be of unestimable worth when obscure mistakes cause trouble later on. Various amounts of program detail may be referenced in the flow chart, thus permitting one to have macro-flow charts which only relate to general areas of the problem and micro-flow charts which provide sufficient detail to permit very rapid writing of the, say, Fortran statements.

6. Prepare a set or sets of test data and calculate by hand methods the appropriate answers. Since you cannot "see" your information in the computer it is necessary to be able to know you get the correct answers.

7. Prepare a "work sheet for variables" and "execute" your flow chart once or twice by entering values of the test data and re-

sults of calculations and manipulations on this work sheet. This step tests the flow and logic of the diagram. Obviously you don't expect the computer to know if your logic or routing is incorrect. Only you can check this, and it is much easier to do with a combination of the flow chart and work sheet.

8. Write the coding. It is here that Fortran or Cobol first enter the picture. If everything was well organized and checked up to this point, this coding step is very rapid.

9. You must at this point rigorously accept the assumption that there are some mistakes in your work—there *always* will be at least a few. Therefore, be prepared. Insert some diagnostic print-out statements at key points in your program which permit you to see what is happening at intermediate points during the execution of the program.

10. Through a media such as punched cards, submit the program to the computer. It will first be compiled, and then if syntactical mistakes were not found in your coding, execution will begin. An example of improper syntax would be an extra right parenthesis, or use of a character combination which violates the rules (syntax) of the language used.

11. Debug the program. This is nothing but a reworking of the earlier steps until the answers that the computer obtains for the test data are identical to those obtained manually.

12. Make the "production" execution runs; i.e., prepare the various data sets (undoubtedly much larger than the test data) and have the answers for these data computed. Of course, this last phase may extend over many years.

I realize many of you are not going to wish to spend months or years living with such detail as I have just described. Hopefully, many of you will have an opportunity to delegate all but the first few steps to someone with less comprehension of your problem but in possession of more programming proficiency. However, this delegation can only be successful if two premises are well in mind:

1. You understand and supervise the complete programming process with enough depth that it is effectively impossible for the programmer to institute his own desires, concepts, and theories.

2. You carry out the first few steps, probably through macroflow charting with such care as to guarantee that complete communication with "perfect" accuracy has transpired between you and the programmer. I stress the word "perfect" because the computer has no intelligence of its own and it will compute completely wrong answers with the same speed as accurate answers and will not communicate to you any information relative to the validity of the answers. Hence, the programmer submits coding to the machine which is always assumed to be perfect. If the programmer has no knowledge of its imperfection, then neither will the computer, and, worst of all, you may not ever know your answers are wrong. The philosophic and sociologic implications of this fact are merely beginning to be felt in our world.

From observation of these 12 steps of programming it becomes rather obvious as to the skills, qualities, and traits required if a musician desires to meaningfully apply computers. First he must be motivated to be a perfectionist. He must love detail and not be willing to settle for the subjective. He will have to learn a little bit about problem organization from a computer point of view, and will find it desirable to become at least a "poor" programmer. Hopefully, he should gain moderate programming proficiency.

Of course, I have omitted the most important criterion. He *must* be accomplished in the understanding of the area of music for which he chooses to apply the computer. It is because of this wonderful fact that none of the truly professional people will ever have to worry about being replaced by computer. On the other hand you must desire to see certain of our information processing tasks replaced by a computer process if you are going to keep alive professionally.

A very significant consideration in your decision to apply computers to music must be the recognition that computer science and the computer industry is very dynamic and even one year's lapse of usage can create considerable obsolescence in your knowledge. This in itself is not serious, but the lack of efficiency that it may cause could establish a roadblock to obtaining grants and to competing with those who choose to stay modern. I do not want to create a scare; nor do I wish to overemphasize this point, but I do want to mention it.

I believe that the greatest advance in computer technology is the so-called time-sharing capability. This is particularly true in the field of music where you must interact with your data. You will find that the results of one analysis are nearly always a stimulation and an insight to the make-up of the next analysis, and so on. Research never ends. Time-sharing permits you in effect to own your own large computer at very small computer prices. From the standpoint of the general purpose digital computer economy, we must follow this route.

What is "time-sharing"? What is meant by "on-line"? What is "real-time"? *On-line* merely means that there is an electronic connection by phones, cables, radio waves, etc., between a console and a computer. Present technology allows the separation of the two by thousands of miles. Only two days ago I used a console in Boston connected to a St. Paul computer. By placing another simple phone call, I could have used a computer in any one of several U. S. cities.

"Time-sharing" infers that multiprogramming or multiprocessing capabilities exist within the computer system; i.e., it appears to the user at the remote console that he has the computer all to himself. Many others have this same feeling all at the same instant. In reality, the computer is slicing its time into very small segments, a segment for each user, and hence is able to do all of the work of the many users.

103

"*Real-time*" can be defined to mean that the time between transmission of information from an on-line console and the time that the response to such information (perhaps an answer) is received at the console is a negligible amount of time from the standpoint of the user, his problem, and his environment. This may be one or two seconds in the case of programming but may only be 1/100 second in the case of a computer controlled electronic organ.

Thus, a real time device is on-line when in use. It may or may not be time-sharing the computer with other devices or consoles.

I have just returned from the Spring Joint Computer Conference where the subject "Is computing a utility?" was paramount. At that conference I saw a normal touch-tone telephone used as a remote terminal to a computer wherein a demonstration suggested that in a very few years there will be 100 million remote terminals in the United States—every telephone user will be able to dial a computer for anyone of millions of purposes. The electronic technology is here now; it is only for the human to adjust to this environment.

Remember in all of our discussions, the key word should be "COMPUTING", not "COMPUTERS"! Or better yet "INFORMATION PROCESSING", not "INFORMATION PROCESSERS"!

There are three types of tasks in the world. They are:

1. Only those humans can perform.

2. Only those computers can do.

3. Those which can be accomplished by both.

Let us rapidly enlarge upon those in the latter two categories so we can vastly increase our enjoyment of those in the first category.

Contributors

Barry S. Brook is a member of the faculty of Queens College of the City of New York.

Charles C. Cook is the Director of Systems and Data Processing at Wheeling Steel Corporation. He was a member of the faculty of West Virginia University when his paper was delivered.

Allen Forte is a member of the faculty of Yale University.

Lejaren A. Hiller is a member of the faculty of the University of Illinois.

Gerald Lefkoff is a member of the faculty of West Virginia University.